Trading Places

Debbie Giggle has over ten years' experience as a writer in journalism and public relations. She lives in Norfolk with her children and house-husband, Paul.

Trading Places

How to reverse roles without
falling out, giving up
or going grey

Debbie Giggle

VISTA

First published in Great Britain 1998
as a Vista paperback original

Vista is an imprint of the Cassell Group
Wellington House, 125 Strand, London WC2R 0BB

Copyright © 1998 Debbie Giggle

The right of Debbie Giggle to be identified as author of this
work has been asserted by her in accordance with the
Copyright, Designs and Patents Act, 1988.

A catalogue record for this book is available
from the British Library.

ISBN 0 575 60247 3

Designed and typeset by
Fishtail Design

Printed and bound in Great Britain
by Cox & Wyman Ltd, Reading, Berks

All rights reserved. No part of this publication may be
reproduced or transmitted in any form or by any means,
electronic or mechanical including photocopying, recording
or any information storage or retrieval system, without prior
permission in writing from the publishers.

This book is sold subject to the condition that it shall not, by
way of trade or otherwise, be lent, resold, hired out, or
otherwise circulated without the publisher's prior consent in
any form of binding or cover other than that in which it is
published and without a similar condition including this
condition being imposed on the subsequent purchaser.

98 99   10 9 8 7 6 5 4 3 2 1

For Paul, Charlie, Naomi, Matt and Sam

Contents

	Acknowledgements	9
	Foreword	11
1	Whose Role is it Anyway?	13
2	The Great Indoors	24
3	The Life of Riley	53
4	Changing Relationships	81
5	Iron Out the Rough Spots	101
6	What the Experts Say	138
7	Protecting Your Rights	151
8	Role Reversal and Early Retirement	166

9	Where to from Here?	175
	References	179
	Useful Addresses	185

Acknowledgements

My acknowledgements in the writing of this book go first to my husband, Paul Giggle, who reversed roles with me in 1992, and gave me both the time and the encouragement to put pen to paper. I also thank Sarah Hannigan and Faith Brooker for bringing the project into print.

This book could not have been written without the help of the many couples who explained their experiences of role reversal, or completed the survey, and I am deeply grateful for their time and trust. I also thank June and Lee for suggesting so many brilliant interviewees.

A number of leading academic figures provided me with quotes for the book, including Adrienne Burgess who invited me to interview her at her home, and Andrew Samuels and Elsa Ferri, who discussed the subject at length with me by telephone. Ian Mackay of Families Need Fathers and Justin Woolf of the Norwich Young Fathers Project provided an important perspective on fatherhood. Thanks also go to Channel 4

Television and the Barrass Company for their excellent programme *Genderquake* and for their permission to publish certain statistics from their extensive research.

On a practical level I am very grateful for the financial advice from John Gaskell BA (Econ) FIFP CFP, and the comments provided by various health professionals, who preferred not to be mentioned individually.

Lastly, I would like to thank our two youngest children, Naomi and Charlie (for keeping things to a dull roar while I typed), and of course Tina Barrett whose friendship, over the last twenty-four years, I have always valued and seldom deserved.

Foreword

When Paul decided to give up work in 1992, to look after our eight-year-old daughter and newborn son, we thought the only thing that would change was our bank balance. Going from two salaries down to one seemed pretty frightening, and we wondered whether we were doing the right thing. Luckily, we have never looked back.

What did surprise us, however, was that reversing roles turned out to be far more than a simple shuffling of income and debts. After about eighteen months we saw that our relationship was changing to accommodate the new way of operating. With our youngest son now on his feet, Paul had little time to analyse, but I became fascinated by this process of change and decided to see whether our experiences were common to any other couples'.

So began an absorbing period of research into an area in which very little information existed. I saw immediately that our situation was far from rare, and that the number of couples reversing roles was steadily increasing. For some the job situation had been a deciding factor, while for others it had always been planned that the man would stay at home. I soon saw that there were a number of reasons why these experiences should be brought together in a book.

First, while much has been made of househusbands, the woman's part in role-reversal had been almost completely ignored. The woman who reverses roles, however, has an enormously important part to play in making the situation work well, and I thought it crucial that women should have a way of accessing the experiences of others.

Second, men who reverse roles are taking a huge leap of faith, and experiences or advice from men who have already made this decision could help couples to assess whether reversing roles would work for them.

I recognize that every relationship is different, and I offer this book with the understanding that each reader will bring to it a unique set of circumstances and a personal vision. I hope however, that among the many experiences and practical suggestions included here, there will be ideas and insights that each reader can use as they trade places.

Debbie Giggle
September 1997

CHAPTER 1

Whose Role is it Anyway?

In today's relationships, having a male or female role all to yourself is something of a luxury. To keep a roof over your head, food in the fridge and the boss off your back, you both have to pitch in. There simply isn't time to put a demarcation line down the middle of the family. If your toddler is about to insert a rapidly disintegrating rusk into your new CD player, you don't say to yourself, 'Looking after children is woman's work, I'll just get the wife.' You take charge and swiftly airlift your little darling to the nearest flip-top bin and baby-wipe. And if the electricity bill is keeping you awake at night, and you're hiding your car in a neighbour's garage until you can afford the road tax, you don't put on your pinny and plump up the cushions in your best imitation of Doris Day. You *both* find ways of boosting the family finances.

We are all, to a greater or lesser extent, sharing the responsibilities for income, home and family, and if there ever was a real dividing line between a man's role and a woman's, that line is becoming increasingly blurred.

We have all got used to women working full time. In fact, statistics say that half of all mothers now go back to work by the time their child is a year old, and the fastest growing group of Britain's workforce is women with children under five.[1] The biggest change to have occurred in recent years is that the person caring for the children while the woman works is increasingly likely to be her partner, instead of a childminder, au pair, nanny or female member of the family, such as a mother-in-law or sister.

A growing band

The latest statistics for the UK estimate that 17 in every 1000 fathers have reversed roles to look after their children while their partners work full time.[2] This would mean that there are around 110,000 full-time dads in Britain. Similar statistics from the Census Bureau in the United States estimate the figure there as 2 million, with the US Bureau of Labour Statistics recording a 26 per cent increase in three years of men aged between 25 and 54 who are keeping house on a full-time basis.[3]

This is probably just the tip of a very large iceberg because the situation is seldom as clear cut as the statistics indicate. In research carried out by Dr Elsa Ferri for the National Child Development Study, nearly 12,000 33-year-olds were interviewed, of which 1,196 were mothers of children under five who worked. 37 per cent of this group said that their spouse or partner looked after the children in their absence – by far the highest percentage. This compared with 19 per cent employing childminders and just 4 per cent employing nannies.[4] When you also take into account the many couples who stagger the hours they work to make it possible for both partners to work and care for the children, we are looking at a sizeable proportion of the population.

Why is the figure so high?

There are a number of reasons for this high percentage. The structure of the job market has changed significantly in the last two decades. In that time in Britain over 2 million men have disappeared from the workforce. In figures for 1995, quoted in the Channel 4 programme *Genderquake*, it was also shown that for every one job gained by men, women gained two. Much of this has stemmed from the growth of traditional areas of female employment, such as the service sector, which account for 97 newly created jobs in every 100.[5]

But employment is not the only factor considered by couples when they reverse roles. In the opinion survey commissioned for this book[6] we put the same questions to 76 people who had reversed roles. They ranged in age from 29 to 54 and had traded places for between one year and 17 years. In each case the woman was the primary breadwinner; the man was a full-time house-husband, was in part-time or self-employment or a student, or was at home following redundancy or early retirement. First, we asked them why the man took a major share in caring for the children.

An important reason was simply the desire not to miss out on a child's development, and 47 per cent said they wanted to spend more time with their children than having a full-time job would allow.

Our daughter Karen is the most important thing in our lives. Neither of us minds working, but at the end of the day we work to live, not live to work. We had no intention of leaving her with a childminder if we could help it and have fitted our jobs around her, not the other way round.
Mark (35), an electrician by trade, caring for Karen (4)

But the deciding factor in the greatest number of cases was the woman's ability to earn more or having the greater job security, with 79 per cent in our survey saying that this was important.

We never really considered any other option. We certainly didn't want to work flat out to pay a childminder, and my wife's job in teaching had the best salary, security and long-term prospects.
John (40), full-time dad for 12 years

For 37 per cent of couples flexibility was the most important aspect, and in many cases the man had the most 'child-friendly' occupation.

Simon's job was by far the more flexible as he is an antiques dealer and can run his business from home. It made much more sense for Simon to combine Jack's earliest years with running his own business.
Sally (43), teacher

Leaving the traditional 9-to-5 job has enabled many men to fulfil particular ambitions or make major career changes, and 31.5 per cent of those interviewed for our survey were combining childcare with other activities, such as full-time study or self-employment.

Colin had always wanted to do a degree in history, but there wasn't the opportunity. When Jacob was born we decided that the time was right, and now Colin studies and looks after him at the same time.
Mette (28), housing officer

Sharing the wage-earning and caring is increasingly popular, particularly where one or other of the parents works on a shift-basis. Of the people interviewed, 10.5 per cent said that work patterns were an important consideration.

TRADING PLACES

Joanna is a midwife and works various shifts, all year round. So although we don't see ourselves as having reversed roles as such, we are certainly able to share the responsibility for caring for Samantha much more evenly between us than we would if we both worked traditional 9-to-5 hours.
Graham (47), antique dealer, who shares the care of his 10-year-old daughter with his wife

In some cases circumstances have imposed a new way of working things out. Of those interviewed, 26 per cent said redundancy and/or a difficulty in finding the right kind of work had affected their decision, while 5 per cent found that ill-health enforced a change in who would be the breadwinner.

Keith was taken very ill a few years back, and the doctors were adamant that he should take things easier and reduce the levels of stress in his life. So we decided that he would look after our two teenage boys and the house, and I increased my hours from part time to full time.
Marlene (49), finance officer

In some cases – around 5 per cent of those surveyed – it just seemed an appropriate time to opt for a quieter life.

I treated it as early retirement, really. I had done well in my career, but after working for over 30 years I definitely felt that I had 'been there, seen it and done it'. On the other hand Debbie's career was just taking off, and there were a lot of things she still wanted to achieve. So it all made perfect sense.

Paul (47), ex-production manager, who has been a full-time house-husband for five years

Big decisions

The reasons for trading places with one another may be absolutely logical, but almost all couples underestimate the impact that this decision can have on their relationship. We may be changing our circumstances simply to make sure that we can pay the credit card bill, but, we are, in fact, changing some aspects of male and female dynamics that are older than Western civilization itself. Although the power balance in your relationship, the pull of gender conditioning and sexual territory may be the last things on your mind when the red gas bill pops through the door, at some time in the future your relationship will almost certainly be subjected to some unfamiliar forces. These pressures may not be immediately apparent, if the research serves us well, but they will almost inevitably surface if you continue your role reversal beyond the all-important 18-month mark.

But does role reversal really change anything? Of the women in our survey, 95 per cent said that they believe there is a significant difference between being a working mum with a childminder and having your partner at home. Equal numbers of men and women – 79 per cent – said that reversing roles changes the way you look at things, and 68 per cent of women believed their relationship had changed as a result of reversing roles, although 74 per cent had not expected it to change.

Interestingly, less than 5 per cent of women who had reversed roles for less than two years said that their relationships had changed as a result, while of those whose partners had spent more than two years at home, the figure was much higher, with 72 per cent saying that they felt that their relationships had changed. Clearly, a certain amount of adjustment occurs when the role reversal continues over a long period.

Will things change for the better?

Happily, 63 per cent of couples agreed with the statement 'We are happy as we are and will change things only if we have to', while 21 per cent said, 'This is only a temporary situation and things could change in the future.' Just 15 per cent plumped for the statement, 'It's not ideal but at the moment we don't really have a choice.'

With hindsight, would they do it all again? The survey found that 79 per cent of men and 84 per cent of women said 'Yes, definitely', while 16 per cent of men and 10.5 per cent of women said 'They'd have to think about it'. Only 5 per cent of men and 5.5 per cent of women said 'Definitely not'.

Other people's opinions are all well and good, but if you have reversed roles yourself or are thinking about doing so, there will be one or two areas you will want to look at in more detail.

- What is it like to be a full-time dad or house-husband?

- How does it change your life?

- What are the potential problems?

- How do mothers feel about leaving their partners in charge?

- How does reversing roles affect your relationship?

- Should you resist change or allow your relationship to evolve?

- What kind of things cause conflict?

- How can you avoid falling out?

- What do the experts say?

- How will it affect your children?

- How can you protect your financial security?

- How does it feel to reverse roles in early retirement?

- What other useful pieces of information are there?

Trading Places has been written to answer these questions. So keep reading.

Chapter 2

The Great Indoors

It's a man's world, they say, so how do men feel about donning the oven gloves and heading for the Great Indoors? Why are they prepared to swap the status and financial independence that come from full-time employment for the sometimes thankless task of full-time fatherhood?

There are only so many ways you can juggle the salary, the childcare fees and the bills before you arrive at the same conclusion. Either one of you works full time to pay a nanny, or one of you gives up completely. In our case it made no financial sense for that person to be my wife, as her job was secure while my company was making many people redundant. To be honest, I never thought I would enjoy it as much as I do.

Mike (34), ex-design engineer, who has looked after Thomas (5) and Polly (2) since birth

I trained as an engineer, but in fact my career followed a very different route, into furniture design and then into sculpture and art. It just worked out that I was home based, while Chris, who is a teacher, was out at work.

Dave (46), father of Siân (17) and Alex (13)

And why is it that so many men, who find themselves looking after the home because of redundancy or unemployment, enjoy the experience so much that scanning the job pages becomes less and less important?

I never even considered the fact that I wouldn't be able to find a full-time job when we moved to the coast. But as time went on, Elaine found work and I didn't. There were plenty of low-paid, part-time jobs, but I couldn't find anything in car mechanics, which is my trade. So we decided to swap roles for about 18 months until Matthew started school. Elaine's job went from strength to strength, so she has stayed the major wage-earner for

the last 17 years. A temporary solution became a happy long-term arrangement.
Peter (54), full-time father in 1980–82, who now runs a window-cleaning business

It seems that it makes little difference whether you choose to reverse roles or have the situation forced upon you. The experiences of full-time dads are strikingly similar, whatever the circumstances, and the following chapters apply equally whatever your initial reasons for heading for the Great Indoors.

Reversing roles can be a big decision, and men will often have a number of concerns, including:

- Can anybody do it?

- How do you learn how to do the job?

- How will it change your life?

- What are the drawbacks?

- How do you overcome the obstacles?

Can anybody do it?

Whether all men can become house-husbands has been much debated by psychologists and the like, and everyone has their own opinions. Our interviewees, however, had obviously met the challenges head-on and believe that looking after the children and the home is not just the province of a woman.

I think you know in your heart of hearts if you can do it or not. I don't think every man would have the patience, and it requires quite a bit of self-sacrifice, so not every man would want to. But in my case I suppose I knew I would be fine.

Steve (39), looked after Luke (10) and Jessica (5) until recently returning to work

My mum was taken ill when I was about ten, and my dad, who was a miner, was at work all day. So I just took over the care of the house and my little sister. When we had our son it never even occurred to me that I wouldn't be able to look after him.

Anthony (37), ex-interior designer/decorator who looks after Jarrad (18 months)

THE GREAT INDOORS

There are some men who you look at and think – no chance – they'll never manage. Women don't have that option. It's expected that they'll cope with a small baby, even if they don't feel comfortable with the idea. Some men and women take to it like ducks to water, while others would rather be out at work. That's not to do with gender, it's to do with your personality.
Dawn (38), bank clerk

You have to realize that you're not just playing at it or standing in for your partner. It's not a rehearsal, this is the performance, and you get the most out of the experience if you throw yourself wholeheartedly into the job.
Paul (47), ex-production manager, who looks after Naomi (12) and Charlie (4)

How do you learn how to do the job?

The consensus of opinion is that learning how to do the job is easy and that you don't need books to explain how to do the housework. However, one or two interviewees put forward some tips that they had picked up along the way and that they hoped would be useful to anyone about to go solo.

Ten tips

- If something is labelled 'dry-clean only' it probably means it.

- Never trust anything dark until you've washed it on it's own and checked the colour of the water.

- Kids' clothes seem to be designed by people who don't have children. Pale pink suede boots, dry-clean only tracksuit bottoms and things with lots of pleats should be avoided at all costs.

- Linings have to be ironed on a cooler setting than the outsides or they shrivel up.

- If you iron thermal underwear it ends up feeling like crisp packets.

- The reason they give babies white chocolate is that the other stuff doesn't wash out.

- Rubber gloves may look stupid but they stop your hands disintegrating.

- If you want to get rid of the smell in the microwave put some lemon juice on a plate and give it 30 seconds on full power.

- Keep an eye on sell-by dates when you go shopping or you may end up with everything having to be eaten on the same day.

- Never admit you know how to sew. You never know where it will end.

How will it change your life?

Of course, everyone's circumstances are different, but there are some experiences that are common to many house-husbands, including:

- greater freedom
- more self-sacrifice
- a feeling of satisfaction
- a change of viewpoint and greater understanding of women
- feeling closer to their partner and children

- initial period of adjustment to get used to the new life

On the negative side, however, many house-husbands reported:

- less time to themselves than before
- longer working day
- a danger of becoming isolated
- less confidence or a feeling that their status had diminished

It's immensely rewarding and the four and a half years I've spent at home have been the best so far. Your life changes completely and that takes some getting used to, but I have no desire to go back to full-time work.
Paul (47)

It felt really strange at first. There was no structure to the day and each day seemed so long. I don't think you realize how much a baby drains you, They're very demanding and everything else seems to fall apart.
Colin (33), full-time student, now looking after two children

When I first reversed roles with my wife it was the early 1980s and it was really unusual for a man to help with the housework. I used to be really embarrassed. At one time the houses on either side of ours were being renovated and there were gangs of builders in. I would wait until they went in for their lunch before I hung out the washing. I was convinced they were laughing their socks off.
Peter (54)

What are the drawbacks?

Of course, role reversal is not an easy option, and there are bound to be some disadvantages to your new situation, so before you make the big step, you may like to think through some of the following points.

- First, how strong are your ego and self-image? It may seem a strange question, but our society undervalues the role of someone who cares for children and the home. Things are similar for men and women in this respect, and you may feel that society has relegated you a few divisions, whether you like it or not. How much will this matter to you?

- What things will you miss most from your working life? As women will tell you, bringing up the children can be hugely rewarding, but there are sure to be gaps to fill.

- Do you have enough support systems? Who can you call on for help and encouragement? Men often approach full-time fatherhood like sailing round the world and insist on doing it single-handed. It *is* possible, but you would have to be mad to try. And not even Sir Francis Chichester would have wanted to spend five years or more on the water.

- How will you replace the structure that full-time work demands? Each day can seem very like the last when you leave the workplace behind.

- Are you really prepared to do your share? Or will the housework still be waiting for your partner when she walks through the door? Can you give this job as much commitment as the last?

- Will your new life make you feel isolated? A large number of your friends could be at work during the day, so where will you look for adult company?

- How will you keep your brain active? There may be those who can find endless intellectual challenge in daytime television and ironing duvet covers, but when the initial novelty wears off, you may need to look for new ways to stretch your mind.

So let's tackle some of the things that trip up the full-time father.

How do you overcome the obstacles?

One point on which many of our interviewees agreed was that your ego can take a bit of a drubbing, not because you are doing 'a woman's job' but because you are no longer seen as being part of the traditional world of work.

Men are often conditioned to see their success as a man as being entirely tied into their success in their career. The image of the successful man as portrayed in television advertisements is a give-away – a new car, a smart house, a beautiful girlfriend or wife, a loud stereo and enough money to buy premium lager – and at the back of it all, you get the feeling that they have somewhere important to go. Characters in television dramas may be policemen, doctors, vets, farmers, dustmen, musicians or market traders, but they are usually employed – with the exception of Rab C. Nesbitt, which rather proves our point.

With this as the perceived norm, is it any surprise that men who leave a 9-to-5 job behind can feel consigned to the substitutes bench instead of taking the penalties.

Being made redundant hit me very hard. It made me realize how competitive men are. It's not really overt, but it is there, and you feel it all the more when you're not able to match them – car for car, Rolex for Rolex. I know it's immature, but it's a way that people measure you, and without a career path you score a big zero.
Michael (38), chartered surveyor

Because people see me around the house and in the village during the day they assume I have nothing to do. In fact, I'm rushed off my feet working from home.
Graham (47)

What really brought it home to me was when a policeman stopped me outside my mother's house for absolutely no reason. He asked me why I was hanging around in the

middle of the day, and said that there had been numerous break-ins in the area. In the eyes of the law I had gone from being a production manager in charge of 250 people to a shady-looking character in just six months.
Paul (47)

There's very little you can do overnight to change the way that society thinks, so you had better make sure it doesn't get to you.

Do's and don'ts to stop the ego from deflating

- Don't believe the hype. The media would have you believe that you need a brand-new, 2-litre, 4-wheel-drive vehicle before you dare show your face in public. It's all nonsense, so just ignore the stereotyping.

- Don't let anyone wear you down. If you've got a mother-in-law, brother or friend who always makes you feel depressed or deflated, keep your distance.

- Don't set your standards impossibly high and don't try to be a super-hero. If the baby screams every time you put him down, don't feel a failure if the dust on the television is an inch thick.

- Don't feel embarrassed to read booklets produced for new mums if you're at home with a young child. Some of the information will be useful. Booklets for new dads, on the other hand, may be less helpful.

- Don't be afraid to get as much sleep as possible. Tiredness can set in very quickly, particularly if children are bad sleepers or are ill. If you get the chance for a nap, take it and don't feel you have to launch into the housework.

- Don't bottle up your feelings. If you're struggling to come to terms with your new situation, discuss how you feel with your partner.

And here are some things you *can* do:

- Find ways of boosting your ego in other ways. Going to the gym or playing in the local football team will allow you to get the aggression out of your system and feeling fitter gives a boost to the ego.

- Think carefully about your ambitions. What really motivates you? Are your ambitions dependent on your career or can you fulfil them in a different way? Think about the proudest moment of your life or the happiest.

Identifying what made it special may tell you something about your true motivations.

- Sit back and enjoy the admiration and envy. Women are full of praise for men who are willing to stay home with their children. In addition, there are many men who would love to be in your position if their finances allowed it.

- Be kind to yourself. Don't allow yourself to be your worst critic.

- Remember that you are providing the best possible environment for your children. The job may not carry a high salary but there is no greater responsibility.

Structuring the day

For many men the most difficult thing to get used to is the lack of structure. After years of managing their time, balancing workloads and dashing to meet deadlines, being at home every day can be a bit of a shock. The day can stretch ahead of you and seem endless.

When I gave up work I went into a bit of a decline. I really thought I had made the wrong decision. It was just

the shock to the system. After a while I was fine.
Stephen (38), who spent two and a half years looking after his two youngest children and is now a full-time student

At first it's a novelty and you think you've got nothing to do but watch the telly. But after a while, you realize that there is a hell of a lot of housework piling up, the school needs your help, the windows need cleaning and the ironing is bursting the door off the airing-cupboard.
John (40)

When I gave up work I told everyone I was going to improve my golf handicap. They bought me a new golf-trolley as a leaving present. But in the last five years I've only played golf about twice! The day may seem really long, but just try finding time for three hours of golf!
Paul (47)

So how do you get used to this completely new way of life?

- Don't let yourself go to pieces. It may be tempting to give up shaving and go out in your oldest track-suit, but it doesn't help your self-confidence if old ladies run away from you in fright.

The Great Indoors

- Don't expect to impose the same level of discipline on a baby or toddler that you could impose on workmates. You may decide to leave at 10.15 a.m. sharp, but chances are you'll realize they have a dirty nappy as you're about to leave and have to stop to change it. On the way down the path they'll hurl their juice-bottle in a muddy puddle and you'll have to go back for a fresh one. You'll get to the car and realize that a shoe and a box of baby-wipes have disappeared somewhere along the route. By the time you've found them, it's 11.05 a.m. and nearly time for the next feed!

- Don't get stuck indoors too often if you can help it. Both you and the kids will benefit from time outside, even if it's just walking to the nearest park and back.

- Don't be concerned if you're writing lists all the time. It goes with the job – shopping, things needed for school, bills to be paid . . .

- Don't be worried if you get to the end of the day and haven't finished any of the things you wanted to do. Sometimes you can be so busy with the kids that everything else falls by the wayside.

And now for some do's:

- When the kids are older set yourself a schedule for the housework. You are more likely to feel relaxed when you've finished your work for the day than sitting in an armchair telling yourself you really ought to do it.

- Hurl yourself into things, even if you would rather be doing something else. You will get more satisfaction if you give it your commitment and take a pride in it.

- Be ambitious. Get out the finger-paints, cook something a bit more adventurous or come up with a new idea of something to play with the children. It will make for a more interesting week and the family will love all the attention.

Isolation and loneliness

A major problem for both men and women when they leave work and spend more time at home is that they can very quickly feel isolated. For men who reverse roles this is compounded for a number of reasons:

- Overall, there are fewer men than women at home with children.

- Most friends will be occupied during the day.

- It can be difficult to fit in to the other set-ups that mums have, such as toddler groups and coffee mornings.

- You can find that you have less to talk about with other men, particularly if their interests are work-related.

- Many daytime leisure activities are set up with women in mind. Very few cater for men with small children.

- You may have less free time than you would like, and your partner may be working long hours to keep the money flowing in.

- You often feel you can't justify the costs of childcare just for your social life.

Some men feel completely comfortable with this arrangement.

I can honestly say that I didn't get lonely. As long as I had the TV, the radio or a good book I was perfectly happy.
Peter (54)

But for others, feeling cut off from the rest of the world can be a problem.

I did take Karen to the parents and toddlers group, but to be honest it felt to me like the Japanese gameshow Endurance! *It was about six months before anyone actually spoke to me. A lot of men feel quite comfortable surrounded by women, but it didn't really suit me.*
Mark (35)

I felt completely isolated. I used to spend a lot of time with my next-door neighbour who had a baby the same age as Morgan, but her husband started to act a bit funny, so I thought I'd better find something else to do with myself. I kept up my rugby and would go to my local pub during the day occasionally, but most of the time I just walked with him in his buggy. We must have clocked up miles over a year.
Sam (38), full-time father in the late 1980s with children Morgan (11), Sam (10) and Rebecca (8)

Our interviewees generally felt that things are improving and that people are much more welcoming to full-time fathers than ever before. However, it can still seem a rather lonely life, particularly during the winter or if you don't have your own transport.

THE GREAT INDOORS

- Find out what is happening in your area. A number of activities are organized for parents and their pre-school children during the week. Try sports centres, swimming pools, museums, local theatres, libraries, parent and tots organizations, etc.

- Give things a try. If you go along to something and feel out of place, nothing will persuade you to go again. On the other hand, you may find that it helps to make the days more interesting.

- Try to keep in contact with friends and maintain the activities you had before. This isn't always easy, especially when money is tight or you are managing without a car, but it will help you to feel more in touch.

- Consider making contact with other full-time dads and perhaps arrange to meet up. More about this in Chapter 9.

And some things to bear in mind:

- Don't worry about how women react. There are more men than ever before who look after their children during the day, and you are likely to be made welcome. Conquer the initial awkwardness and join in. Many men say that they have been made extremely welcome at mother and toddler groups, National Childbirth Trust coffee mornings and so forth and enjoy the company.

- Don't forget that your child's primary school will probably be grateful for any help you can give if you find yourself with time on your hands.

- Don't forget that you may be able to arrange a couple of hours of childcare in the week to give you some time to yourself. Do the sums and see whether this is possible, or consider organizing a rota with neighbours to share the load.

Support systems

Everyone needs help at some time or other, particularly if the children are small or if you are trying to work on a part-time basis. Don't be afraid to think this through and have a list to hand of people who will help if required. All too often men, even more than women, think that they can do the job single-handed.

After about a year of carrying my toddler around I had real problems with my back. Eventually I was laid up for

THE GREAT INDOORS

six weeks. There was no way my wife could get the time off work, but luckily my mum was able to step in.
Paul (47)

I'll never forget the day that I had to rush Morgan to hospital, when his younger brother knocked a heavy piece of furniture over and it crushed his toes. If my neighbour hadn't been there to take the other kids off my hands I don't know what I would have done.
Sam (38)

Support system checklist

Can any of these help?

Mother or mother-in-law

Father or father-in-law

Sisters or sisters-in-law

Brothers or brothers-in-law

Friends

Neighbours

Other mums or dads whom you know from your child's school

Play groups

Nurseries

Childminders
Au pairs
Baby-sitters

Keeping your brain active

Even with the best will in the world you are bound to miss some of the intellectual challenge of being in full-time work. How can you replace this when you reverse roles?

I guess I was lucky in a way, because I kept working. I'm an antiques dealer and before Jack started school he went to all the auctions with me. It can be difficult to juggle the two things, and switch from remembering when the next bottle is due to bidding for a particular lot, but I wouldn't have wanted to give up completely.
Simon (39), antiques dealer

Here are just a few suggestions for things you can do to make sure your mind doesn't atrophy completely:

- How about a new area of study? You can choose the level of commitment to suit yourself, from a degree with the Open University to a one-day workshop on being your own boss. Many areas have advisers on adult training opportunities, and individual colleges will also help. Some courses are subsidized, but overall the costs are reasonable, and many colleges now reimburse GCSE or A-level course fees if you pass the final exam.

- Get practical. If the thought of having to paint a skirting-board or change a tyre makes you feel ill, this could be the chance you were looking for. Practise some of the skills you always wanted to develop.

- Get creative. There has never been a better time to finish that novel that has been lying in the bottom drawer of the desk, or get a sketch pad and pick up where you left off at school.

- Follow the markets. Start to track share prices and read up on what is happening in the world of investments. You don't have to put your money at risk – set yourself a fantasy share portfolio and track it's performance over a year.

- Play guitar like Hendrix. If you've ever wanted to do it but never had the time, now is your chance.

- Give your career a thorough work-out. If you were less than happy before you gave up work, now is the time to reappraise your career path. Work out an action plan to get you where you want to go and strike off in this completely new direction. If you're changing careers, the most difficult thing is showing experience or aptitude for the area you want to move into, so perhaps you could use this time to work on a voluntary basis to improve your chances of a full-time position later on.

- Could your past work experience help other people? You might enjoy being a school governor, a volunteer on a conservation project, a treasurer for the rugby club or an adviser for young entrepreneurs. Numerous organizations would be grateful for your time.

- Read all the books you have never had time to read. This is easier said than done with a small baby, but it will keep your brain ticking over.

- If all else fails, there is always a cookery course. There are worse things to do than wile away the hours over a hot stove.

The best (and worst) things about being a role-reversed dad

Our thanks go to the dads who contributed the following:

The worst bits

- Cleaning up sick . . . and worse.

- Women always telling you their problems.

- Hearing the baby crying yet again in the night and knowing that only a bomb would wake your wife.

- Finding that house-husband doesn't exist as an occupation.

- Finding that all your T-shirts have grease-stains down the front because you won't wear an apron when you cook.

- Having to watch the Shopping Channel in the middle of the night because it's the only thing on when your hyperactive two-year-old is wide awake.

- Always having to be Father Christmas because you're the one with the deepest voice at play group.

- Never having the chance to spend thirty minutes on the loo.

- Forgetting yourself at a dinner party and cutting up your wife's meat for her.

- Launching into a conversation at the pub about what was on mid-morning television and then realizing that everyone else was at work at the time.

The best bits

- Seeing all of Wimbledon/the Olympics/Ryder Cup from start to finish.

- Sitting down with the paper and a cup of tea in the morning.

- Never missing sports day or the Christmas carol concert.

- Never having to take a dressing down from anyone.

The Great Indoors

- Going back to the things you loved doing when you were young, such as kite-flying, fishing, and playing with Scalextrix and train sets.

- Being able to admit that you don't give tuppence about career progression.

- Not having to drive up and down the country trying to sell photocopiers.

- Having more than your fair share of holidays.

- Never being at the mercy of a mobile phone or pager.

- Spending summer afternoons in the garden with the kids in the paddling pool, a cold beer in one hand and a good book in the other. Not just the odd afternoon, but week after week.

Chapter 3

The Life of Riley

It is obvious that reversing roles will change a man's life entirely, but surely the same cannot be said for a woman. It's just like being a working mum but with less housework, isn't it?

Strangely enough, reversed-role mums tend to agree that employing a nanny or childminder differs enormously from role swapping with your partner. Obviously, there are enormous benefits.

When we were both working I felt permanently exhausted. We only had one car so everything had to be planned like a military operation to get Lucy to the childminder and both of us to work. I remember one morning I was absolutely screeching at Lucy to put on her socks and I

suddenly thought, No money in the world is worth this. Something has got to give. We don't find it easy to manage now financially, but I feel we've got our priorities right and we're all much happier.
Katherine (34), midwife

Colin worked really long, irregular hours after Jacob was first born. It became steadily more difficult to organize everything. We had huge rows when we were together and my job started to suffer. I loved my job, but I just couldn't handle the work load the way I wanted to with all my other responsibilities. My employers were brilliant and very supportive. I eventually asked for a demotion to a job with less stress and they allowed me to move to a different role in the organization. Since Colin gave up work, everything has slipped into place. Jacob is really flourishing and I'm back on top of my job again.
Mette (28), housing officer

Perhaps it's just us, but we had really bad luck with nannies. They were all great with Emily but they were so unreliable. We had one who went on holiday and never came back . . . No warning . . . No letter . . . Just an absence of childcare on Monday morning and one furious boss. In just three years we had a whole stream of them and sometimes they weren't even honest. At one stage Philip and I were sitting up until midnight every night with Emily and the nanny swore that she hadn't had a nap all day. We later found out that the nanny was cuddling her to sleep for three hours every afternoon so that she didn't have to play with her. You think it's really easy to employ a nanny and leave it at that, but there's so much stress it really isn't worth it. Since Philip gave up work that all seems like a bad dream and the problems we had with Emily disappeared almost overnight.

Elena (38), merchandising manager

But is being a role-reversed mum a bed of roses? Does it mean that, as many people imagine, you can lead the life of Riley? All the mums in the survey agreed that reversing roles has meant the best of all worlds for the children, but many said that there are certain sacrifices they had to make and new pressures that come into play when you reverse roles.

They agreed that you have to ask yourself a number of questions:

- How will you feel about letting go of the mothering role?

- How much will the opinions of other people matter?

- Are you ready for the responsibility of being the breadwinner?

- Will it change the person you are?

- Will it affect your career?

- Will it affect your relationship with your child?

- Will it change your relationship with your partner?

Learning to let go

One of the most difficult things about being a role-reversed mum is learning to let go. Many couples reverse roles without realizing that their relationship with one another and with their children will almost inevitably change. Women, in particular, underestimate the impact that this will have on their lives.

If your partner is going to fulfil the traditional mothering role you have to make room for this to happen, but women are often possessive about the way their children are brought up. Perhaps as an extension of their maternal instinct, they see it as their job, and as their ultimate responsibility. Some women, after all, build their entire lives around their homes and families. But if your partner is giving up his job, his place on the career ladder and, very often, his social status, you need to give him the space and authority to do the job in his own way.

That may seem absolutely logical, but thousands of years of civilization and a lifetime of conditioning seem to blur this logic, and even the most forward-thinking of us arrives at this point with some pretty unwieldy stereotyped 'baggage'.

The overwhelming realization of role-reversed couples is that there are two natural roles in parenting – one of providing food and shelter and one of nurturing and caring for the family. Each role is independent of gender, so our traditional view of male and female roles is actually a misleading one. Indeed, the roles are interchangeable, and many couples swap backwards and forwards between the roles throughout their lives as parents. But in the same way that men worry they might be less of a man for doing women's work, the woman can often be made to feel less of a woman for letting go of the mothering role. And while it is applauded when a man helps to care for his children, it is sometimes frowned upon if a woman allows him to take this responsibility out of her hands.

The process of letting go can be a painful one, as many women find themselves caught between making the situation workable on a practical level and reconciling the way that they feel about relinquishing the mothering role. Those who have made the transition advise that you should let logic win out over conditioning and learn to delegate.

How do you delegate successfully?

One of the first rules of management is, if you delegate a task, don't go back and interfere with the way it's done. It will only demotivate the people carrying out the task and prevent them from learning how to tackle it well. It will also turn a loyal supporter into a new enemy.

When we consider how effectively most of us delegate in our working lives it is surprising how thrown we are when we need to apply the same simple rules at home. So many arguments and hurt feelings stem from this aspect of reversing roles that it almost deserves a chapter to itself.

When you have your first baby everyone is bombarding you with advice on what you should do, and it takes all your energy to stand on your own two feet and make your own decisions. Before you know it, you've taken on the whole mothering bit and you try to be an expert. You feel less of a woman somehow if you can't cope or if the baby yells all day and you don't know why. For the first couple of years I always felt that Harry was ultimately my responsibility even though Craig had given up his career to care for him. So I kept trying to stamp my authority on everything Craig did. It must have been soul-destroying for him. Slowly I started to let go of the responsibility but it was a long time before I could feel good about it.

Cheryl (36), marketing manager

The first day I went back to work after maternity leave I left a great long list of instructions for John because I was convinced he wouldn't know what to do for Robert. Every day I mapped out his schedule for him. About eight years later I found out he had just buried my instructions in the nappy bin every morning and gone his own sweet way. I suppose I believed that only women could look after children properly. It was hopelessly old-fashioned to think that way. Anyone who spends day after day with

a small child learns how to look after them. It's not a matter of male or female. It's a matter of practice.
Sue (38), teacher

I work in human resources so I have a fair bit of practice of things like delegating, and I was determined not to break all the rules when Steve started looking after Joel. Right from the moment Joel was born Steve took over the main role of caring for him. It wouldn't have been fair to dominate the baby completely for four and a half months and then drop Steve in at the deep end when my maternity leave finished. Unfortunately though, a few people assumed that I did this because I had rejected the baby or that I couldn't cope. I think they thought I was a bit cold or unfeeling because I didn't snatch the baby away from Steve the minute I walked through the door, criticizing him for not being able to look after him properly. It's almost as though that was what they were expecting. You get used to being misunderstood when you're a role-reversed mum. People can understand what it must be like for a man, but no one understands what it feels like on the other side of the coin.
Hilary (29), personnel officer

Sometimes I really have to bite my tongue. I wanted to stop sterilizing bottles sooner. I would've started solid food earlier and as for potty training . . . Well Callum would have been dry a year earlier if I'd had my way, but when I tried to put my foot down it led to a real row. Eventually, after a particularly heated exchange, my husband told me that if I wanted to give up work and do the job myself I should bloody well do it. If not I should get off his back! I didn't like it at the time, but I realize now that I wasn't being fair.

Helena (41), company director

Do's and don'ts of delegating

- Start as early as you can, particularly with a small baby, so that the person staying at home can set his own routine.

- Take your lead from your partner. If he wants a completely free hand try to support him, even if it means biting your tongue now and then. If he is uncertain about his new role, be more actively involved until you see him wanting to call more of the shots.

- Try and make as many of the landmark decisions together, such as when and how to potty train.

- Let go of a little of the responsibility at a time and feel comfortable with it. If it all happens too quickly you might suddenly feel redundant until you find new ways of fitting in.

- Remember this is his full-time job.

- Remember that the traditional 'mothering role' is a stereotype. No one actually lives up to it, so don't feel guilty if you're not super-mum. Look at the average new man with a stay-at-home wife. That's a more appropriate role model – if you feel you need one.

- Remember that the child doesn't really need two people to carry out the 'mothering role'. Think about how you can balance the part of the 'fathering role' that your partner doesn't have time or energy for.

- Find one special time or activity that is always yours. Some women always bath the children. Others always organize birthday treats. Make this 'yours' in the eyes of the children and make room in your working life to enjoy it.

- Make up your own mind. After all, parenting is an inexact science and all relationships are different.

- Talk to your partner about how you are feeling. If he is struggling to come to terms with a new way of life you may be the last thing on his mind. If you don't tell him how you feel he may never think to ask!

And now for the don'ts:

- Don't forget how difficult the job is. If he's spent all day chasing (unsuccessfully) a two-year-old with a potty and the laundry basket is full of wet knickers don't say: 'Its not difficult, you know. My sister's baby was dry at 15 months.'

- Don't destroy his confidence. Being a role-reversed dad is enough strain on the ego as it is, without your criticizing the way he looks after the children.

- Don't take back a job once you've delegated it. It is guaranteed to irritate and demotivate.

- Don't worry what other people think. Their views are probably out of date. Few people understand the situation unless they have been in a similar one.

- Don't delegate every single household chore and expect him to wait on you hand, foot and finger! It could cause all sorts of problems.

- Don't forget that we all have our bad days. Feelings like guilt, jealousy and even resentment of your partner are absolutely natural reactions and are experienced by many. If you start to feel any of these uncomfortable reactions to your situation, don't turn them inwards. They are probably just a sign of the strong feelings you have for your children and your devotion to their well-being. Try to see things positively and work round them. See Chapter 5, Iron Out the Rough Spots, which looks at some of these problems.

Silencing the critics

Putting your relationship on a comfortable footing when you first reverse roles can be tricky, but unfortunately, not all role-reversed mums are able to draw encouragement and support from the people around them. Quite the opposite in fact. Many report that mothers, in-laws, friends and others often make the whole thing more difficult by questioning or even openly criticizing the new arrangement.

I think in our case it made a strained relationship even worse. My sister-in-law and I have very little in common.

TRADING PLACES

She hasn't worked since her children were born and sees me as a bit of a mercenary go-getter. When we reversed roles she flatly refused to believe that Steve had done so of his own free will. It's been a while now, but she still thinks I forced him into it. I must admit we see less of them now than we used to.
Hilary (29)

We can't win really. My mum thinks John is too lazy to work and insists on telling me how unfair she thinks it is that I have to work so hard. On the other side of the coin, my mother-in-law thinks I have bullied John into staying home to further my own ambitions. You would have thought that, after 11 years, they would have got used to the idea!
Sue (38)

An old friend and I always used to tell one another our problems over a pot of coffee or bottle of wine. But since I reversed roles everything has changed. When I moan that I never get any time to myself or complain that it's been a pig of a week, I can see that her sympathies actually lie with my husband . . . and not with me at all. The problem is, your viewpoint changes. For example, the first time I saw Shirley Valentine *my sympathies were with the wife, but when I saw it again recently I thought the*

husband was really hard done by! It's no surprise that even the closest of friends can't make that transition with you, unless they have reversed roles themselves.
Katherine (34)

Do's and don'ts to silence the critics

- Don't pay any attention. This may be easier said than done, but you really can't afford to worry about other people's opinions. Be firm and confident and leave them to it.

- Don't take an aggressive stance. Setting yourself in the blue corner and your sister-in-law in the red corner will just make the situation more uncomfortable.

- Don't feel you have to justify yourself or prove anything. People may stand in judgement, but that doesn't mean you need to be judged.

- Don't forget that humour can ease the situation. Brushing up your repertoire of mother-in-law jokes might not, however, be a good idea.

- Don't ever take sides with one of the critics to get a little sympathy. Even after a week from hell, it is not a good idea to sob down the phone to your mum that you've made a terrible mistake. Your partner is the one to confide in. If you have doubts, discuss them together.

- Don't resort to 'well you're a fine one to talk . . . ' Reminding the critic of the shortcomings of their own relationships may be extremely satisfying at the time, but will fuel the argument like paraffin on a barbecue.

So what can you do?

- Try to diffuse the situation if you can. If you refuse to rise to the bait, the potential scene will probably just fizzle out.

- Ask yourself why it's important to you that people approve. If you actively need their support, is there another way round it? Can anyone else provide encouragement or help or have you just got used to pleasing people to keep the peace? Are you acting out of habit?

- Remember that the loudest critic could also be the greatest fan. Often the mother-in-law who snatches the tea-towel out of her son's hand and casts horrified sideways glances at your shop-bought Christmas cake, is the same person who brags endlessly to her friends about her unique son, attributing his domesticity to her skills in bringing him up. This phenomenon is strange but true.

- Keep lines of communication open at all times. It is better to clear the air than to set up a stony wall of silence.

- Remember that people have no right to pry. There is still a curiosity value attached to role-reversal, but the right to keep your life private remains with you at all times. Be firm if you feel people are overstepping the mark. Don't feel bullied into telling people how your relationship works.

- Bear in mind that even the most conventional of relationships have their critics.

- Feel proud of your achievements. Celebrate the landmarks – for example, have a role-reversal anniversary or a romantic meal to celebrate the youngest child starting school. There's nothing like a celebration for making the critics eat their words.

Being the breadwinner

Apart from learning to delegate and having the odd critic to contend with, being the breadwinner is a bed of roses – right? According to the vast majority of women, not quite.

You may let go of one set of responsibilities when you reverse roles, but you instantly take up another. When a full-time wage disappears from the monthly income it can give you a bit of a jolt. No matter how comfortable your finances, suddenly assuming sole responsibility for the security of your family can take some getting used to. Most women have grown up with the idea that they will look after themselves or contribute to the joint wage, but the concept of supporting your children as well as an unemployed adult single-handedly was not part of the plan.

I didn't really notice how heavy the responsibilities felt until Paul got a job for three months over the winter to help out. It was almost like someone taking a huge rucksack off my shoulders.
Debbie (35), public relations consultant

There were talks of redundancy at my company recently and it was terrible. I was absolutely terrified that it could

be four or five months with no money at all, while I tried to get another job.
Hattie (26), marketing coordinator

I know it's terrible to say it, but I can understand why some men just take off and leave their wives. The pressure on you can sometimes seem so great that you can imagine what it must be like to just wash your hands of it and walk away.
Alison (40), journalist

The thing that really plays on my mind is that Colin would really struggle to step straight back into a senior management job on the same salary he had before. He's 50 now, with a five-year career break on his CV. There's no guarantee that he could earn anything like the salary we need if I were to lose my job. That's a sobering thought, you know. Once you go down this particular path it can be really difficult to turn back.
Brenda (45), company secretary

So what are the kinds of question you should ask yourself when you become the breadwinner?

- How far ahead have you been planning your career? Many women have not considered a straight run through to retirement. Does reversing roles mean you should reassess the direction you are taking in your career?

- Is there a chance that your desirability as an employee will drop as you get older? Some careers, such as those in the computer industry and in advertising, have a preference for employing the under forties. Look at the job advertisements for age limitations and check with specialist recruitment agencies. Should you be thinking about new qualifications or skills that will give you greater flexibility to change careers if necessary in future years?

- How long will this situation continue? Most couples know that they can exist on one salary for only a certain amount of time before their savings run out and the debts rise. Most just cross their fingers and hope for the best, but if you estimate a sensible target date it will put a 'light at the end of the tunnel' if you need one at any time. If you manage to keep going longer you will have another reason to celebrate.

- Are there other things that you should be doing to safeguard the family finances? You don't need to go overboard and buy every kind of insurance that you can, but there may be basic levels of protection that would be advisable. Don't forget that in many circumstances your partner will have to discontinue his pension, if he is no longer a tax-payer. See Chapter 7, Protecting Your Rights, for more information.

- You are more important to your family than ever now, so how are you going to look after yourself? Think about your overall health and fitness. Give yourself time to relax and find out about stress-management techniques. Most women feel so guilty that they are leaving their partner in charge that they work themselves to a frazzle and let their health go to pieces. This doesn't benefit anyone.

- Take a look at all those overweight, underinsured men in dead-end jobs. If men have managed all this time without reading advice from self-help books, it can't be all that difficult to be the breadwinner successfully. In fact, you will probably beat them all at their own game.

Career questions

Once the decision is made, the role-reversed mum can concentrate on her work. The experiences of women in their working lives vary enormously – there are those who thrive on every minute, while others would give their right arm to swap back if the finances allowed.

There is absolutely no doubt that I would not have been offered the directorship without the added security of a house-husband. Competition is so fierce that the smallest concern in the corporate mind can consign you to the side line. It may be a cynical viewpoint, but in my opinion, for many companies a woman with a house-husband is the best possible option. If you're married but childless you keep getting embarrassing questions until you're safely past the menopause. If you've got a nanny, bosses are often nervous that you will let them down. Jobs involving large amounts of travel are often barred to you. If you're single or divorced then you get sideways looks as though you're about to waylay the next single man and frog-march him up the aisle in a headlock. All in all I think my domestic situation has enabled me to reach heights I could not have otherwise considered.
Helena (41) company director

But not all women feel that having a house-husband liberates them to this degree.

I know that I would have taken more chances with my career if John had been the higher wage-earner. I would have moved more frequently and in teaching very often the only way to move up the ladder, is to move schools. But the timing was always difficult, and I couldn't risk a bad decision.
Sue (38)

The problem I found wasn't so much the childcare, but the pregnancy and maternity leave. I was completely healthy right through my pregnancy and took the minimum maternity leave, but I still lost a lot of status. I was passed over for promotion and lost my annual bonus. More importantly, junior employees who reported to me tried to 'mother' me while I was pregnant. I found that really patronizing and it undermined my position in the bank.
Sarah (29), banking professional

Many employers have made a real commitment to improving job prospects for women who have children and return to work, but in case you have to look after your own interests during this time, the following may be useful.

Do's and don'ts for maternity leave

- Make sure you understand your basic rights. It may be deeply boring to mug up on employment law, but it could make all the difference if you have a maternity leave pending.

- Think through how the employer is likely to react to your good news. Look at how they have handled recent situations with other staff and plan accordingly.

- Don't forget your intrinsic worth in the job market. Pregnancy is not good for the career ego, but check the salaries across the board for your qualifications and experience and keep those in mind should your status start to slip with your waistline. You need to be confident when you negotiate your arrangements.

- Don't panic if you feel your career is sliding back temporarily. Even the most patriarchal company can't ignore real talent and commitment. With your partner taking care of your domestic responsibilities, you can begin to dazzle and confound.

Relationships with the children

Some of these points may seem a bit worrying, but don't be discouraged. Although your life may be changing, role-reversed mums are in agreement that the essentials do not.

For the first few years I absolutely tortured myself for no reason. I was convinced that my son wouldn't love me any more or that he would forget about me. A colleague said that she felt the same way and worried that her baby would become too attached to the au pair. It didn't make me feel any better. You can sack an au pair, but you can't sack your husband! I had read all this stuff about bonding and was convinced that I would always be an outsider. I needn't have worried. Charlie and I are really close and I never doubt that he loves me as much as his dad.

Debbie (35)

I don't suppose my relationship with the boys is a classic mother/son relationship. It's much more like the father role. I used to read the bedtime stories and later on I helped with the homework (until the maths got too

difficult). One thing I really like is that they are always pleased to see me when I get home at night. When you're at home with them all day you can become part of the furniture.
Heather (46), charity administrator

I don't think you really give anything away in the long run. The day-to-day handling of the household is one thing, but the love they have for you is quite another. Relationships are more complex. They go deeper than the actual mother/father stereotypes.
Chris (38), teacher

None of the mums interviewed had long-term concerns about their relationship with their children. Many were sad that finances dictated that they had to spend time away from the children, but the consensus was that there is absolutely nothing to fear.

The top 10 best (and worst) things about being a role-reversed mum

Many thanks to the mums who contributed the following:

The worst bits

- School fêtes. Your husband knows all the mums and chats away for hours while the dads strike up conversations with one another about work. You're left standing at the bouncy-castle, minding eighteen pairs of trainers and without a soul to talk to.

- Having to slog your way to work on a boiling-hot day when the family is taking a picnic to the park.

- Seeing the disappointment on young divorcees faces when you turn-up with your partner on sports day. They thought he was widowed/divorced/available and hate you to bits.

- Realizing you don't know how to operate the electric oven any more.

- Feeling completely remiss when you fail to recognize your son's teacher in the supermarket and then can't (for the life of you) remember her name!

- Losing all credibility with your children when you don't know Charlie Chalk and can't identify characters from Australian soap operas.

- Having to do the ironing because your partner melts all the buttons and shrivels the linings.

- Receiving a verbal warning for keeping expressed breast milk in the office fridge.

- Moving mountains to get a day off work to go to the Nativity play, and the school changes the date at short notice.

- Knowing that you always miss them more than they miss you.

The best bits

- Going to bed after a Sunday evening dinner-party and leaving the washing-up.

- Not having to sit through the same video over and over again with your three-year-old.

THE LIFE OF RILEY

- Being allowed a snooze on a Sunday afternoon.

- Buying Lego at Christmas and knowing that you won't have to spend every day picking it up off the carpet.

- Not only being able to do your job but being able to plan as well.

- Not having to watch the clock during afternoon meetings in fear of having to make an embarrassing early exit.

- Not having to pay the equivalent of a mortgage every month for your childcare fees.

- Not having continually to rack your brain for something to cook every night.

- Being able to spend the weekend with your partner doing something other than cleaning, shopping, washing and so on.

- Knowing that the person looking after the children is the only other person in the world who loves them as much as you do.

CHAPTER 4

Changing Relationships

We've looked at how reversing roles affects the individual, so now let's see how it affects the relationship. First, does it really make any difference?

When you reverse roles you bring about a fundamental change in your relationship. I don't think anyone realizes how big a step they are taking. Because it makes financial sense it just seems logical, but I think you need to consider the ways in which it will change your life.
Felicity (43), police officer

Perhaps I was naïve, but I didn't really expect anything to change. We had always shared the responsibility for

the house and the children, so I didn't see that it would affect us. But about 18 months after we reversed roles, some really basic things in our relationship started to change. The ground was shifting and there were things we had to deal with before we could stabilize things again.
Debbie (35)

The things you expect to happen don't really come to fruition – you think he won't be able to set the washing machine and he has no problem at all. But there are other things that you don't expect, that are much more about who you are and how your relationship operates. Even if you're not the sort of couple who sit and talk things through all the time, you have to be prepared to discuss how you feel and make sure that each of you knows where you stand.
Diane (36), insurance clerk

Why should things change?

It seems that, on a temporary basis, reversing roles makes very little difference to the dynamics of the relationship. If you change places for a sustained period, however, the impact can be noticeable.

TRADING PLACES

When a couple reverse roles they are, in essence, changing the way they handle their joint responsibilities. Certain jobs and pressures are handed from one partner to the other, and this changes the whole shape of this external part of their relationship. The stresses and strains of everyday life fall in different places, but although the shape of external responsibilities is radically different, the inner relationship remains unchanged. 'That's great,' you may say, 'we wouldn't want our relationship to change, just because we do things a bit differently.' But the reality seems to be that no relationship is static and immobile. Relationships are dynamic and flexible and will begin to grow and adapt to find more comfortable ways of fitting into the new set-up.

During the initial period of transition it can seem as if the relationship is being pulled in different directions. There may be conflicts and the couple will find themselves re-establishing some fundamental cornerstones of their relationship. That doesn't mean to say that all couples will start yelling at one another – indeed some may glide along without noticing anything at all – but many couples have been through this period of transition. The more easily the relationship adapts to it's new environment, the shorter this period of conflict or instability seems to be.

Later, the relationship seems to stabilize again in a new format, which mirrors it's external responsibilities.

What causes the changes?

You may be changing the responsibilities in your relationship, but why should that make any difference? In the time that you have been together, your relationship has undoubtedly grown and evolved already. Why should reversing roles be any different, for example, from the changes you experienced after you both became parents?

We posed these questions to our interviewees and asked them to analyse the factors at work during the first few years of role-reversal. Three important points arose from these discussions:

- The power balance
- Conditioning

- Ultimate responsibility or in other words 'Where the buck stops'

In this chapter these factors are explained in more detail, while in Chapter 5 we look at the sorts of problems relationships might encounter.

The power balance

It appears that relationships often achieve an internal power balance. Some relationships rattle along quite nicely out of balance, but most modern couples tend to prefer an even distribution between the partners.

This balance is arrived at through a complex set of factors such as emotional need, fidelity, assertiveness and strength of personality, and the happiness of each partner can often be linked to it. Power within the relationship is at it's most obvious when there is an argument, as many rows are caused by one of the partners trying to tip the balance in their favour, to the disadvantage of their partner.

Here are two fictional examples to explain this concept more clearly:

Example 1
Jane is fed up. The football season has started again and John spends two evenings a week and

Changing Relationships

all day Saturday playing football. He hardly ever sees the children and Jane has no free time at all. She has had enough and tells him so. They have a huge row. John says he works long hours and deserves time to himself. Jane isn't happy, as she works too but doesn't get a moment herself. John is expecting to have the lion's share of the fun and free time at her expense. This tips the balance in his favour.

Example 2
Jenny has been on yet another shopping spree and has taken her credit card up to its limit. Tom can hardly believe she has been so stupid when they already owe so much on personal loans and mortgage arrears. She tells him he's just mean. By relying on her partner to do all the worrying for both of them, Jenny is tipping the scales in her favour, instead of striving for a balance.

People exert power over their partners in many ways. It could be by forcing decisions or abdicating responsibilities or acting out of self-interest. This applies in traditional and role-reversed relationships as well as in other forms of interaction, such as between mother and daughter, or boss and employee. The following points could help you to analyse how a power balance is achieved in your own relationship with your partner.

- Cast your mind back and try to remember the last five arguments you have had with your partner.

- Try to pin down exactly what it was all about, e.g. money, family, lack of consideration, and so on.

- Who felt upset enough to start the argument? Which of you felt they were getting a rough deal? Did you each have an equally valid point? Or was one partner exerting power over the other?

- Who came out on top, and why?

- What does this tell you about the way a balance of power is achieved in your relationship?

As relationships evolve, the balance of power is continually being negotiated, and when we reverse roles one extremely important deciding factor changes – earning power.

History has shown us that the partner with the earning capacity can tip the power balance in their favour very easily, if they choose to do so.

Changing Relationships

Until recently the balance tipped in favour of the man in almost every case. In some countries little has changed in this respect, but in most parts of the Western world, a significant trend of the last 30 years has been the growing financial independence of women. This has been one of the factors that has evened up this balance of power and given women more control over their own destinies. The phrase 'equal opportunity' encapsulates this power balance between the sexes.

What we see in the role-reversed relationship is the potential for this balance of power to fluctuate, changing the traditional position of each partner. If we bear in mind the complex strands from which equilibrium is established in the early stages of a relationship, it is reasonable to suppose that a change in the power balance can send even the most established relationship into a bit of a spin.

Much of the way in which a relationship evolves derives from this shifting power balance. Couples need to acknowledge how it is affecting their relationship and bring it back to equilibrium. In Chapter 5 we look at the conflicts that can be caused when the power balance starts to shift and suggest some ways of dealing with the problems.

Conditioning

We believe that we are living in an enlightened society. We give our daughters cars to play with and encourage our sons to express their feelings. If you suggest that people have been conditioned to expect certain things just because of their gender, you are likely to be accused of old-fashioned thinking and even sexism. None of us, however, is completely free of conditioning, and when we reverse roles we are vulnerable to all sorts of preconceived ideas. There can be a gap between the reality of our lives and what 'seems right'.

Even when I was a little girl I expected to have a career. I wanted to be financially independent and have a more varied and interesting life than my mother. But if I'm honest, I didn't expect to have two children and work straight through to 65 with only eight months off. I suppose I thought that being married would change all that somehow. It didn't really occur to me that my life would be more like my father's than my mother's.
Sue (38)

Changing Relationships

I loved every minute of looking after Matthew while Elaine was at work, but somehow it always seemed wrong. At the back of my mind was a nagging feeling of guilt that I should be bringing home a big salary instead of pegging out the washing. I couldn't ever feel at ease with myself.
Peter (54)

I have always seen myself as the beer-drinking, rugby-playing man, and I don't mind admitting that I struggled to come to terms with being a full-time father. After about 18 months I had really had enough of being at home with a small baby. If we hadn't employed a nanny when we did I think I would have lost my sanity.
Stephen (38)

Reversing roles puts couples into circumstances they have not been conditioned to expect. We haven't grown up with the idea of carrying out the opposite role, and elements of the new set-up can seem unnatural. This legacy of 'how we see ourselves' can apply pressure on the relationship, and it can lead to confusion about how each partner fits in to the new set-up. Without the traditional guidelines we are conditioned to expect, we have to invent new ones as we go along. People can find themselves struggling with ideas of their own identity, and each partner can feel guilty or out of step with what society regards as the norm.

Ultimate responsibility

An important element of reversing roles is the apportioning of ultimate responsibility for the care of the children and the home. In some relationships the man will take on the chores associated with the job, but will not carry the ultimate responsibility. In many cases women refuse to let go of the 'territory' they see to be theirs, while men often lack the confidence to take it on.

Transferring ultimate responsibility is a much more fundamental change than just transferring tasks such as vacuuming and washing-up. It appears to be the pivot around which the relationship revolves. If the man remains a 'caretaker' of the role, with the woman holding the reins, the situation is likely to last only for so long before something gives. Either the man will be miserable and give up, or the woman will burn out with the effort of trying to carry too much responsibility. At this stage it appears that the couple will either find a completely different set-up – employing a childminder, for example, – which allows them to go back to their original roles, or they will tackle the issues and find a way of making the situation work, which will lead to them reversing roles entirely, with the ultimate responsibility passing to the man.

This period in the relationship can be very short – a matter of months – or it can last for several years, but while it is working itself out, the lines aren't clearly drawn and the relationship must find a way to function day by day. If both sides want the responsibility and neither is willing to give any ground, the happy home can seem more like a war zone.

It takes confidence on both sides and consensus from both partners, but where the responsibility lies is really the crux of reversing roles and dictates whether the relationship will evolve from where it is now or return to where it was before. It certainly cannot remain in limbo for too long. Chapter 5, Iron Out the Rough Spots, looks at this subject in more detail.

How does the relationship change?

Every relationship reacts differently to role reversal. It can create a better distribution of power and strengthen the bond between the couple, but it can put weak spots under considerable strain. In most cases reversing roles occurs around the same time as other major developments, such as the birth of a new baby or changes in financial or work circumstances, so the relationship often has to cope with a bombardment of changing conditions. This can lead to differences of opinion, hurt feelings, resentment or disorientation, and although the situation can be resolved with discussion and compromise, it can be uncomfortable at the time.

I don't think you can rely on reversing roles to save your marriage. You have to really be prepared to find solutions and not just score points. You have to keep talking and retain your sense of humour at all costs.
Felicity (43)

You have to look out for the niggles in the relationship. If you don't you can end up with a full-blown row on your hands. Toes are often trodden on and egos are regularly

bruised but you need to be sensitive to how your partner is feeling. Don't trivialize their views.
Marlene (49)

It's important to realize that what is happening is being driven by what's happening outside. It doesn't touch the chemistry that brought you together in the first place. You need to work together to get the outside right, not rip the inside apart.
Sally (43)

Should you resist change?

Deciding whether to hang on to what you are and how you see yourself or whether to adapt to fit the new situation is very difficult.

On the one hand, although you may want to adapt to changing circumstances, there may be areas where you want to limit the impact of the changes. For example, if the power balance swings too far, the woman could exploit her partner's goodwill, complaining that her husband gives her the same filling in her sandwiches every day. Or the man can become a nagging husband

and whinge if the woman doesn't meet his exacting standards around the house.

When you're caring for a tiny baby full time you start to lose your identity entirely. You become a kind of walking placenta and only seem to exist to care for them. It's a really weird feeling. I've talked about it to women at mother and toddler group and they have very similar experiences. But for a man, losing your identity can be quite scary, especially when all the things that made you a macho man seem to dissolve away. As the baby gets older you separate again, and they become more independent. Then you can get back to normal. But I think it's important to lose yourself for a while. It's this bonding bit that they tell you about. I think it happens for men as well as women.
Paul (47)

I think if we were starting from the beginning again I would leave less to chance. Even if it came to drawing up a kind of list of who was expected to do what. I'm sure it would smooth the way.
Stephen (38)

How can you help your relationship to adapt to it's new situation?

CHANGING RELATIONSHIPS

- Keep talking. Sometimes if things are really busy, you can forget that you need to find time to talk.

- Be sensitive to what is happening in the relationship. If you bury your head in a newspaper you could miss the cues. You need to stay aware of how you feel and how your partner feels.

- Stay flexible. If you fight change every step of the way the problems will never be dealt with. Keep an open mind and don't be afraid to rethink things if necessary.

- Take feelings of resentment seriously. Women often resent having to go to work and miss out on time with their children, while men often resent having to go to their partners for money. There will be practical ways round these problems, so don't suffer in silence. See Chapter 5 for more detail on this.

- Play fair. It's easy to exploit your new situation by throwing your weight around or by not keeping up your side of the bargain. Ultimately, this can be very destructive and you don't want to find too much resentment or ill-feeling building up within the relationship, because it could be difficult to diffuse later on or your partner may decide to play you at your own game, and the whole thing will escalate.

- Make sure that you get to the root of a problem. It may be a disagreement about how to close the cereal packet correctly but it could be part of a much bigger issue. What is really going on here? Are lots of small niggles really part of a larger change that needs to take place? Chapter 5 looks at some of the most common areas of conflict in role-reversal relationships.

- Try to keep your temper and never lose your sense of humour.

- Remember that children are very sensitive to their parents' moods. If lots of things are changing round them, they need to feel as stable as possible. If that means staying happy and sunny until they are safely asleep in bed, try to do it, no matter how difficult that might be!

- Remember that it's a joint decision and everyone should try to make it work. There's no room for 'This was all your idea!'.

And now for a few definite 'no-nos'

- Don't allow things to fester. If you ignore a problem it is more likely to grow than go away.

- Don't sulk. Talk about what is wrong. Sulking takes lots of effort and achieves nothing.

- Don't be scared to give things a trial run. It may seem a little cool and calculating, but it gives each of you a chance to see whether something will work before you commit yourselves.

- Don't trivialize your partner's feelings. It may seem totally unimportant that you've left toast-crumbs over the work-surface every day for the last three months, but if it has become a source of constant irritation then you need to take it on board and wipe them up before you go to work!

- Don't expect your partner to take everything in his stride. He has feelings that get hurt and an ego that will bruise easily, so make allowances.

- Don't forget that you will have good days and bad days!

- Don't force your opinions down your partner's throat. You can't dictate how someone should feel or how he should act. The relationship has to be a continual process of discussion and consensus or it just won't work.

- Don't get discouraged. Couples experience pressures on their relationship during a temporary transitional stage. Regard them as growing pains, not as a deterioration.

- Don't involve other people in your changing relationship. There is nothing worse than asking friends round and expecting them to act as referees while you try to resolve your differences. You won't be the first person to ask an embarrassed dinner guest 'Well, what do *you* think Simon? Should I clean the loo or should it be Patrick?' Try to sort it out without an audience.

- Don't try to score points. It may make you feel better to browbeat your partner, but you should be looking for consensus, cooperation and mutual respect. If you're marching up and down the lounge, giving a triumphal salute, the chances are you haven't quite achieved this!

Changing Relationships

- Don't forget that you can go back to how you were before and nothing will be lost. In fact, being more analytical about your relationship and what makes it tick will probably make it stronger. Any difficulties you experience now are likely to be growing pains, and they don't mean that your relationship is falling apart.

Chapter 5

Iron Out the Rough Spots

For most of the time we co-exist quite happily with our partners, sharing the responsibilities and pulling together. Every now and then, however, we have a difference of opinion or tempers become frayed, and before we know it we're glaring across the breakfast table and muttering how inconsiderate they are through gritted teeth.

This doesn't mean it's the end of the world, but these warning bells should definitely not be ignored. Those who never have a cross word are invited to move straight on to the next chapter, but for the rest of us, who find that the path of true love never runs completely smoothly, this chapter may be helpful.

What's the problem?

Every relationship has it's good and bad times, but what kinds of thing cause conflict in the role-reversed relationship? Is it really any different from a traditional father-at-work, mother-at-home set-up?

Each relationship is different, with it's own dynamics, but as was suggested in Chapter 4, there are a number of factors at work in the role-reversed relationship that can cause some uncomfortable moments. These include:

- The power balance
- Conditioning
- Ultimate responsibility

What problems can the power balance cause?

It appears that within every relationship there is an in-built balance of power. This is arrived at over time and is a kind of unspoken agreement as to how each partner should treat the other.

Arriving at this power balance can require a

fair bit of bargaining, with each partner exerting power over the other to ensure that their own practical and emotional needs are met. This can involve practical power such as earning capacity, or emotional power, such as love, support and flattery that your partner needs to feel good about him or herself.

Once this balance of power is achieved, the equilibrium is maintained by abiding by this unspoken agreement and obeying all sorts of unwritten rules. These may be important rules like 'no one should take off to Marrakech with the contents of the joint building society account' or smaller things like 'Mum deserves a night out with the girls once every three weeks'.

When you reverse roles you are changing the type of power which each partner can exert. The woman now has major financial bargaining power, while the man has a greater power over the way in which the family operates. Needs are changing, bargaining power is in different hands. This can lead to a rewriting of the unspoken agreement between partners with a whole range of rules to be reviewed.

Hopefully, the partners can reach agreement quickly and easily, but there is the danger that, instead of finding equilibrium once more, the balance can tip too far in favour of one of the partners.

If one partner is getting an easy life while the other is becoming increasingly disgruntled at what they see as a raw deal, then the sparks will really fly.

What happens when the power balance tilts?

No relationship, one hopes, will experience all of the problems outlined in the following pages, but it may be useful to check that none of these is creating mischief in your household.

Half-a-job dads

It's very easy for men to not notice those jobs that women would normally do. If the pedestal of the toilet is always cleaned while you are out playing football on Saturday afternoons, you might have the impression that it never gets dirty and must be made of self-cleaning ceramic. Many women start to get tetchy when they feel that men are overlooking jobs. Whether men don't notice or choose not to notice is impossible to say, but this can be a very common area of conflict.

- Talk to one another about what each of you is willing to do and what you expect of the other.

- Identify the jobs that neither of you wants to do and come up with some suggestions of ways to get round each one. You could have a couple of options – you could leave it, take it in turns, pay someone else to do it or find a way of avoiding it – buying clothes that don't need ironing, for example.

- If you think it will help, formalize which jobs each of you will do by writing a list or rota and deciding how much time each of you is prepared to devote to housework on top of your main job – the office or spending time with the children, for example.

- Ask yourselves whether certain jobs are actually necessary or are just habit. It would be silly to do a job every week if once a month would do just as well.

And now some things *not* to do:

- Don't forget that if you have a small baby or active toddler around they can completely

Iron Out the Rough Spots

absorb you and leave little time for anything else. If you are having disturbed nights it could be to everyone's advantage if the one at home sleeps when the baby sleeps rather than struggling around the house with the vacuum cleaner. Be sensible about it. Do what really needs to be done, but don't forget how time-consuming childcare really is.

- Don't forget that if you have time to watch daytime television from start to finish with no interruptions you've got time to dust and tidy the sitting room.

- Don't forget that if you become a full-time dad, that the ultimate responsibility for the house lies with you not your partner. If you're clocking up five hours of sports television a day and no one ever has clean clothes for work or school, it's *you* who should be doing something about it during the day not your wife when she comes in from work.

- Don't think that four hours pottering around in the shed makes up for four hours of housework. If your partner comes home from work every night and cooks and cleans until midnight, she is not likely to appreciate your hand-crafted wine-rack. In fact, she is more likely to set it alight on your hand-built barbecue.

Workaholic mums

Freed from the constraints of domestic arrangements, many women throw themselves into their jobs heart and soul. Career success and financial security are more important than ever when you have a single wage instead of a joint income. But for the man at home, the day may seem very different. When you were both working and you got home at 8.30 p.m. you were probably greeted with a kiss and a take-away curry. If you arrive home at 8.30 p.m. now you are likely to be greeted by a burned dinner, a screaming baby and a slam of the door as your partner locks himself in the bedroom to sulk for several hours.

It isn't easy being at home with children day after day. As you mutter angrily under your breath about the supreme sacrifice you are making to keep a roof over the family's head, you must appreciate that there are two sides to this particular problem.

- Put yourself in your partner's place. Children are wonderful, but they are also incredibly demanding and can exhaust even the most devoted parent. It takes two to create them and two to look after them, so working every hour of the day will not help.

- Try to keep your working life in proportion, particularly if you have a small baby at home. Employers are placing a very heavy load on their staff, and this can often mean covering a work load that would previously have been carried by two people. Your employer is not going to do much about this in the short term, so you must find strategies for balancing work and home. By all means work hard, but accept that you have limits and don't feel you have failed if you cannot meet every deadline.

- Be brave enough to look for greater flexibility in your work environment. Can you move your working day forwards or back to make the best use of the time you spend with your family?

And here are a few don'ts:

- Don't forget that people around you may be able to help. People don't always take kindly to picking up mundane tasks from you, but there may be learning opportunities for colleagues in your current work load that they would be happy to lift from your shoulders. Perhaps involving them in certain areas could be beneficial to both of you, if this is agreeable with your employer.

- Don't try to play the company social life like a single man. That may be the way to get on, but the cost will be very high for your family. Just because that's the way men have always done business, doesn't mean that that's how it's got to be.

- Don't drive yourself too hard. Analyse where the pressure is coming from to put in long hours. Is it really coming from the boss or are you actually driving yourself to stay longer?

Female 'chauvinist pigs'

An interesting phenomenon can occur if the woman decides to tip the power balance firmly in her own favour. Many women find the novelty of having someone take over the household chores extremely gratifying. There is a natural tendency for the person who is at home to put their needs to one side to care for the other people in their lives, and many women find, as generations of men before them have found, that this is a pleasant position to be in.

As long as both partners contribute equally to the well-being of the family everything is fine, but if the woman expects to be waited on at every turn a very disgruntled man will soon have something to say about it. It's an easy trap to fall into, and if you do, the repercussions can be serious.

- Before you reverse roles list all the things you wouldn't put up with from your partner – for example, leaving dirty clothes on the floor, complaining about what's for tea and walking around toys instead of picking them up and putting them away. Each month, check whether you have been accused of any of these. If you have, you are slipping.

- Offer to help but don't take over. Pick up any jobs you feel will help and you will be absolutely fine. Supervise him and you might end up wearing the supper instead of eating it.

- Resist the temptation to sit down with your feet up and a newspaper over your face when you get in at night. You might have had an awful day and it might feel like bliss to sit in front of the TV while the man in your life juggles a stir-fry, child two's homework and a bottle of cream cleaner, but ultimately you would be better offering assistance until domestic order is restored.

- Model yourself on the 'new man' with a stay-at-home wife if you want to get the balance right.

Nagging husbands

Men are naturally territorial we are told, and when a man becomes a full-time dad that territory becomes the home and children. How the man exerts his authority in his new-found kingdom needs some careful thought.

When John was working from home he seemed to take over the kitchen. I came home one day and put a wet umbrella on the work surface and he went absolutely crazy at me. It was the first time I'd felt like a stranger in my own home!
Hannah (40), public relations consultant

I'm always being nagged for not doing things properly. First, he doesn't want the saucepans stacked like that, then he moans that I've bought the wrong kind of margarine. Every single time we go to the supermarket he reminds me to collect the £1 coin deposit for the trolley. Every time, every week for the last four years! I have a very responsible job, but he treats me as though I am completely incapable of existing without him.
Dianna (36), company director

Iron Out the Rough Spots

The other day we were about to go out for a walk and we were wrapping up the kids because it was so cold. My husband said to me . . . You'd better run upstairs and put another jumper on or you'll be complaining you're cold when we get round the corner . . . He would never have said that before we reversed roles. He says he just cares about us all, but sometimes he's like an old mother hen. It drives me barmy.
Alison (40)

- Listen to yourself occasionally. Beginning to sound like your mother or mother-in-law may not be a good sign.

- Remember it's a home, not ICI or the armed forces. Look carefully at your management skills and decide if they are appropriate to your new environment.

- Allow your partner freedom to do things her own way. Imposing your standards and methods of working on her may not be the best way to maintain a happy home.

On the other hand:

- Don't become too house proud. By all means get a sense of achievement from what you are doing, but don't make everyone's life a misery by setting impossibly high standards.

- Don't be too territorial. You may feel that you deserve sole rights over the use of the kitchen, but no one should feel that areas of their own home are out of bounds.

- Don't criticize your partner's efforts, even if you believe the results are below the required standard. If you find fault each time, assistance may not be forthcoming again.

- Don't turn into a mother hen. You can become so used to caring for the children and pets that you start to adopt the same approach with your partner. She's a big girl now, don't forget, and may not appreciate your little reminders to brush her teeth and not to speak with her mouth full.

What problems does conditioning cause?

If you maintain a power balance in your relationship that suits you both you can avoid many of the everyday niggles and potential fall-outs of reversing roles, but there is another factor that can sometimes make mischief in your relationship.

Reversing roles has become an option only

since equal opportunities legislation and continual lobbying made it possible for women to earn enough to support their families. Most of us grew up in an environment where men were the main wage-earners while women cared for the home, and no matter how much we may feel ourselves to be free of these constraints, conditioning can cause problems.

The main difficulties stem not from the practical side of reversing roles but from the emotional side. We can tell ourselves logically that this is the best solution, but psychologically we often struggle with some preconceived ideas of who we should be and what society expects of us.

This often manifests itself in a feeling of uneasiness. Somehow everything feels wrong or you feel out of place. Another largely hidden, but potentially destructive reaction that may surface is resentment. Even though we tell ourselves that this resentment is petty and unworthy of us, the strength of conditioning can make it difficult to banish it from our relationships.

Women and conditioning

Young women have been brought up today with the understanding that they can expect everything from life. The sexual revolution of the 1960s and the boom in opportunities for women have opened up a broad and varied range of experiences, which women see as their right – career, motherhood, travel, sexual compatibility. We move into adulthood believing we can have it all.

Inevitably, however, it's not that simple to have everything and lose nothing. The reality entails a kind of juggling, which many women accept as the best way forwards. Working women juggle their career, family, health, leisure and other elements throughout their lives and here we see a fundamental difference between the working mum and the role-reversed mum. The working mum maintains a hold on each of the elements of her life and juggles them, while the role-reversed mum has to find it in herself to share certain 'birth-rights' with her partner. And this can be difficult.

On one hand, a woman may see all the practical advantages of her partner being at home with the children, but on an emotional level it is extremely difficult to let go of something that is so much a part of her status as a woman – being the most important figure in your baby's life.

Of course, this desire is felt by working mothers who resent having to leave their children with nannies or childminders. They can feel enormous pangs of guilt, and the relationship with the nanny can become strained. But for women who reverse roles, if there is resentment, it can actually be directed at their partners, and while childminders and nannies can be dismissed, partners are there for keeps. The child's father is also, possibly, the only person your child might ever love as much as you.

When resentment builds up between the two partners it can be very difficult to diffuse.

You know that it's petty and you try to put it out of your mind, but if you've had a really bad day it can get the better of you. I was at work one day and when I phoned my five-year-old son he said he'd had the best day of his whole life. He'd been kite-flying with his dad. I don't need to tell you how that made me feel – knowing I had missed out yet again.

Mette (28)

It's ridiculous to say that you can be jealous of your own partner, but I so wanted to see Jack do things for the first time. If he said a new word or reached a new landmark while I was at work I felt this little jab of resentment. It soon went away luckily.

Sally (43)

TRADING PLACES

I have always enjoyed working but sometimes I ask myself . . . Why me? . . . Why do I have to keep working until I'm 65? You can't help thinking that way sometimes. It would be really good to retire early, but that isn't an option at the moment.

Marlene (49), finance officer

- Recognize the feelings when they occur. Accept them for what they are and try to understand what has caused them. Often there are certain things that make you feel left out. If you know what these 'triggers' are you may be able to avoid them or just anticipate and rationalize them.

- Make your partner aware of how you feel. Many women feel so guilty or embarrassed about these feelings of resentment or jealousy that they keep them secret. Strong undercurrents operating beneath the surface of your relationship could lead to conflicts in the future, so make sure he understands how difficult you sometimes find the situation.

- Remind yourself of all the good things that are coming from your hard work. Financial security and a safe environment are essential for children as they grow.

- Remember that the child isn't swapping one parent for another but is actually benefiting from two loving and committed parents and getting a double share of attention and involvement.

And now for the don'ts:

- Don't feel that you are being petty. Resentment is an absolutely normal emotion that is experienced by almost all role-reversed women. It will come and go, and as time goes on you will find new ways of handling these feelings. It is springing from the most admirable of emotions – your love for your child – and as your child grows you will see that your relationship is just as special.

- Don't let these jabs of resentment distance you from the family. Men often feel like this in traditional relationships, and they take too much of a back seat in the lives of their children as a result. Hurl yourself into your family life. Spend time with them, and don't ever disappear off in a sulk, wanting them to seek you out. Your role is absolutely crucial, so don't allow yourself to feel pushed out.

Men and conditioning

A man who would happily give up his career to look after the children and the home can hardly be described as an old-fashioned chauvinist, yet, despite the full-time father's ability to welcome a more enlightened approach to fatherhood, conditioning continues to play a part. But how does it manifest itself in everyday life?

I suppose I was worried at first that people would think I was a bit of a girlie. When I told one of my colleagues at work that I was going to leave work to look after my baby he said: 'What do you want to do that for? Are you a poof or something?'
Paul (47)

I'm a member of our local Lifeboat crew, and when I happened to mention that I was staying at home to look after the kids the other crew members just couldn't understand it. It was completely beyond them why any man should want to do it.
Steve (39)

The assumption is that men will struggle with the 'female' nature of the job. Strangely enough, men soon cast off the traditional male stereotypes with hardly a backward glance.

Being a house-husband gives you an understanding of how women must feel, but it doesn't really change how you see yourself. It doesn't make you feel any less of a man. Your sexual identity is much too ingrained to be affected by what you do during the day. That's like saying men who work as industrial cleaners turn into homosexuals. I can honestly say you don't become more feminine when you reverse roles.
Paul (47)

What can happen, however, is that men can feel out of step with what society expects of them. There is increasing pressure on men to see themselves as an integral part of the world of work. Much of their success as a man is tied into their success in their careers, and while most take the whole thing in their stride, this feeling that they 'should really be doing something else' can linger on. But for many, breaking away from this image is extremely liberating.

In the interviews carried out for this book, many of the men had aspirations and ambitions that did not necessarily require the backdrop of a 9-to-5 job. It can hardly be coincidence that so many men were able to follow up areas of interest, such as full-time study or self-employment, which they could not have considered without the stability of their partner's wage. The freedom afforded them by their working partners enhanced their career fulfilment rather than diminishing it. As a result, few struggled with losing the trappings of a traditional man's life.

There is, however, an area of conflict that seems to be affected by the conditioning of our upbringing.

I never used to worry about money before I started looking after Jack. And in a way I suppose I didn't really need to worry. We weren't going broke or anything. But having Jack around when he was small meant that, for the first time in my life, there were limits on how much I could earn. I felt I didn't have as much control over our finances, because there were limitations on my earnings. Feeling that you are not the master of your own destiny is a bit alien.
Simon (39)

I have never got used to going to Diane for money. I know it's stupid, but it never seemed right. I was brought up to be financially independent and support my family, so it still feels embarrassing to ask her for money for shopping.
Mark (35)

Iron Out the Rough Spots

Do's and don'ts for men and money

- Consider a joint bank account if you don't already have one or arrange a regular transfer into the man's account. Many men feel uncomfortable asking their wives for money, and this can be a practical solution.

- Make sure that each of you can access cash in an emergency.

- Try to maintain the system you had before for dealing with money. If the man always went to the bar or paid for a meal, set up your finances so that this can continue. It isn't by accident that people fall into these habits. It has a lot to do with the unwritten rules of your relationship, so don't change more than you have to.

And also:

- Don't trivialize the importance of getting your cash concerns right. Money is a classic arguing point, so don't ignore problems as they arise. Discuss them and try to solve them.

- Don't forget that women who say 'I earn it all, so I'll spend as much as I like' are asking for big trouble! This can make a well-known hot-spot flare out of control. Try to agree on spending rather than flexing your wage-earning muscles.

Where does the buck stop?

Perhaps the most difficult area of all is sorting out who should be doing what. Particularly in the early days of reversing roles, the two sides can refuse to reach an agreement. A little discussion and logical thinking can put much of this to rights as we saw earlier in this chapter. But there is a larger issue to be discussed here, around which the role-reversed relationship will pivot.

At some stage the ultimate responsibility for the children and the home must pass to the person who is in the best position to devote him- or herself to them. A woman would never be happy to do the household chores while her husband had the ultimate say over what she did each day and how she should do it.

The same applies to the man at home. The situation that seems to work most effectively is for the man to accept and carry the ultimate responsibility for what he is doing, while his partner helps and supports him. Sounds like a perfect relationship doesn't it?

But somehow when we reverse roles some strange things happen and this ideal set-up goes out of the window. Instead of a happy, fulfilled man deciding what to do in his own domain, with a loving and supportive partner, we have all sorts of strange permutations and great grey areas of misunderstanding. And it all comes down to that old problem – ultimate responsibility or 'where does the buck stop?'

The problems of ultimate responsibility

This is a complex area and we are working in a largely unresearched field, so we have to make a few intelligent guesses about what is happening in the role-reversed relationship. A theory is that the conflicts come from two main areas – confidence and territory.

If everything is to work as well as it can, the woman has to have confidence in her partner. She must know in her heart of hearts that he can do the job as well as she could. In turn, the man must have complete confidence in his ability to do the job effectively.

In addition, the woman has to be prepared to give a certain amount of territory to her partner. This territory is the area of responsibility for her children that is often seen as hers alone. She must be prepared to share the space she occupies in her children's lives with her partner and, in turn, the man must be prepared to share the territory without forcing her out of her relationship with the children.

What a balancing act it all is, needing so much cooperation, discussion and mutual respect to make it come out right. Many couples reverse roles and never look back, but what can you do if you run into stormy weather?

The confidence trick

You can't magic up confidence out of thin air, yet the relationship desperately needs confidence on both sides if it is to work well with reversed roles.

If a woman doubts her partner's ability to manage, although she may go off to work and leave the children with her partner, she will continue to carry the responsibility for everything for an indefinite period. She will not be able to relax in the knowledge that her partner can really run things in her absence. Over a short period of time the relationship can absorb this lack of confidence, but in the long term there are a number of things laying in wait to trip her up.

- Few women will continue indefinitely to carry the responsibility for both roles. Many single parents manage admirably if there is no choice, but if the woman has a partner she will soon start to feel that the responsibility is a heavy burden, unfairly borne by her.

- Resentment can easily set in if the woman feels she is carrying an unduly heavy burden of responsibility. She can start to react badly when faced with housework or cooking at the end of the day and could blame her partner for her general feeling of unhappiness.

- If she starts off with a lack of confidence in her partner this is likely to continue unless something actively happens to change things.

- Conditioning gives us the ultimate get-out clause. She can say: 'Well, it's a woman's job anyway so how could I expect him to be able to do it?'

TRADING PLACES

Now lets look at things from a man's point of view.

If a man doubts his ability to cope he will fight shy of taking on greater responsibility or, if he does, he will 'refer to the expert', his partner. Over a short period the relationship will absorb his lack of confidence and in many cases the man's growing familiarity with looking after the children will solve a lot of problems. But if his confidence doesn't grow in the long term the following sorts of thing may happen:

- The man feels the role to be temporary and will not give it the commitment needed to make it work. He may not take a pride in it, so will take little pleasure in the results.

- The man becomes disheartened and demotivated. Instead of taking on the challenges and enjoying the experiences, he will start to wish he was in an environment that gave him more happiness and greater satisfaction.

- In real terms, the man's confidence is destroyed by continual 'overseeing' by his partner and what he perceives as her criticism. Alternatively, he becomes angry with her insistence on telling him what to do and how to do it and this will cause conflicts.

Iron Out the Rough Spots

- Conditioning gives him the ultimate get-out clause. He can say to himself: 'Well, bringing up children is woman's work, so she can just get on with it.'

In such a role-reversed relationship we find ourselves in a 'Ring of no-confidence' and the ultimate responsibility stays with the woman, when it would benefit everyone if it could pass to the man. Something like this happens (see opposite).

Downward spirals

If a relationship gets caught in this kind of vicious circle it can be difficult to make role-reversal work. But why can't it work? Surely, if one of you knows what you are doing that's enough. It does seem a bit baffling when we look at it from the point of view of a relationship, but when we apply well-understood management theory, we can see immediately why we run into problems.

For those who have spent time managing other people or studying personnel issues the word 'empowerment' may be called to mind. The belief in management circles is that unless people feel they have ownership over the task they are carrying out they will fight shy of taking on responsibility for it and will rely on someone else

TRADING PLACES

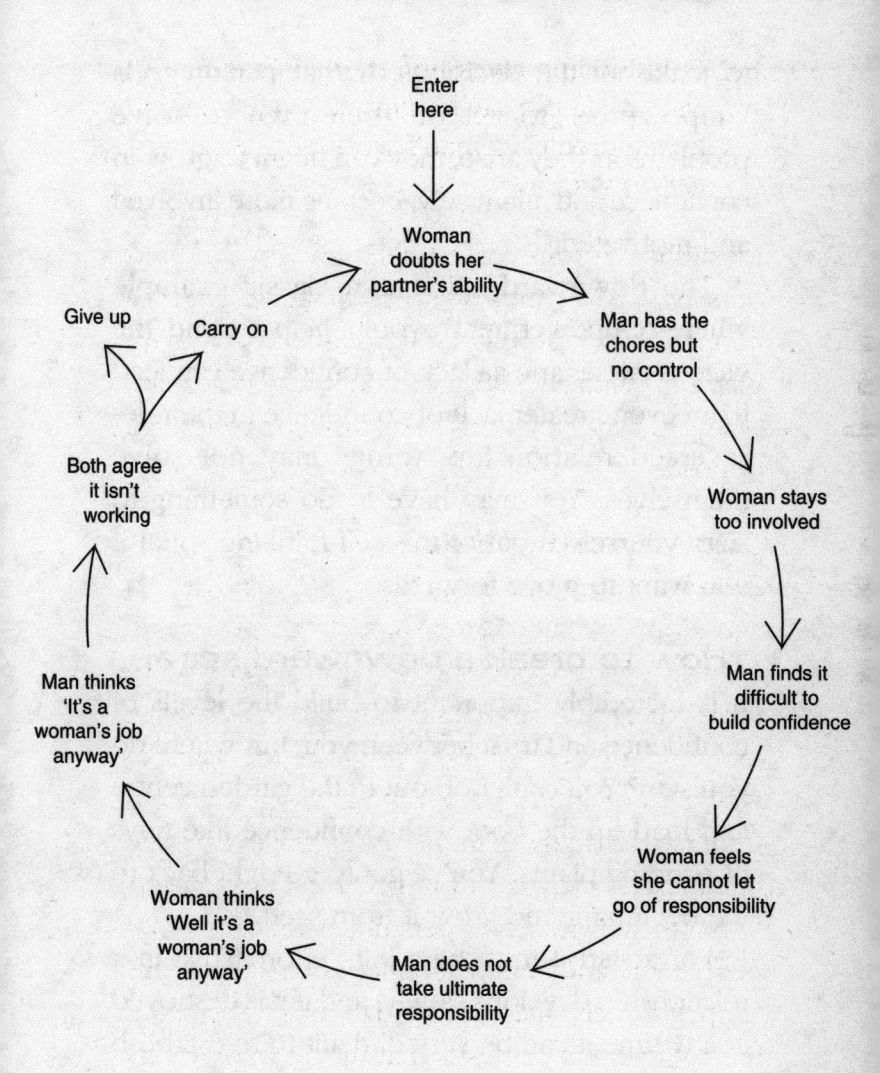

```
                    Enter
                    here
                      ↓
                   Woman
                doubts her
               partner's ability
    ↗                                ↘
Give up   Carry on              Man has the
  ↖    ↖                         chores but
                                  no control
   Both agree                         ↓
   it isn't
   working                       Woman stays
      ↑                         too involved
                                      ↓
 Man thinks
 'It's a                        Man finds it
 woman's job                    difficult to
 anyway'                       build confidence
      ↖                               ↓
   Woman thinks                  Woman feels
   'Well it's a                 she cannot let
   woman's job       ←          go of responsibility
   anyway'          Man does not        ↙
                    take ultimate
                    responsibility
```

The Ring of No-confidence

to make all the decisions. If that person feels 'empowered' to act on their own to solve problems as they arise, they can begin to grow in confidence and, ultimately, become more involved and motivated.

The downward spiral is a classic example where 'empowerment' would help to end the vicious circle, and as lack of confidence can lead to an even greater lack of confidence in the role-reversed relationship, things may not solve themselves. You may have to do something to snap yourselves out of this self-fulfilling spiral if you want to move forwards.

How to break a downward spiral

It is incredibly important to build the levels of confidence and trust between you, but where do you start? You can't pop out to the garden centre and load up the boot with confidence like trays of bedding plants. You've got to go right back to the beginning and grow it from seed.

For a start it must be a joint effort. Trust in a relationship develops slowly, and if it is destroyed at any time it can be very difficult to re-establish it. If you are aware of what's happening, you can develop confidence, even from the shakiest of beginnings.

Do's and don'ts for women

- Help your partner. He will need your whole-hearted support, particularly in the early stages.

- Be prepared to bite your tongue occasionally. If he's struggling to undo a BabyGro – all fingers and thumbs – don't say, for example, 'Oh for goodness sake give him to me before you drop him on the floor.'

- Do start early. Begin to involve your partner as soon as possible. If he learns alongside you with a new baby, confidence will develop well on both sides.

- Remember, if he obviously is not coping, that he needs your support not your criticism. Show him that you don't doubt his ability but look for practical ways in which you can improve the situation. Do beware of taking things back, though. See Chapter 3 on delegating.

And the don'ts:

- Don't forget that your partner has nothing to prove. He won't be getting a mark out of 10 at the end of the week. He said he will take on the job and it's not for you to judge him.

Iron Out the Rough Spots

You would find it absolutely intolerable if you thought he was judging your capabilities as a parent, so apply the same principles with him.

- Don't let people around you destroy his confidence. Give him your complete backing, and if you have doubts keep them to yourself.

- Don't expect miracles overnight. It takes time to adjust to a new role.

- Don't lose your sense of humour. Babies are incredibly tough, so if he's put the nappy on wrong and there is zinc and castor oil all over the baby's feet, there will probably be no ill effects. It's not worth throwing a fit about.

- Don't be lulled into the conditioning trap. Many women feel that haranguing their partners for doing things wrong is almost expected of them. This is old-fashioned stereotyping.

- Don't be tempted to relate his domestic disasters to a delighted audience when you're out together. His flushing a disposable nappy down the toilet and flooding the bathroom may be a wonderfully witty story, but he may not appreciate you narrating it to his mates at the rugby club. If he chooses to do it, that's different.

Do's and don'ts for men

- Have a go at everything. If you always wait for your partner to do something you may never learn yourself.

- Refer to books or magazines. It's how lots of women learn. She may be a bit unnerved when you come up with ideas of your own, but you should be playing an equal part in this.

- Remember that if you're doing things properly it should be a full-time job. If you're spending four hours a day watching television you are probably missing a chunk of it.

And now for some don'ts:

- Don't forget you are the master of your own destiny. The job is yours now, and you have the capability of loving or loathing it.

- Don't forget that practice makes perfect. If your first attempt at something fails, don't give up.

- Don't forget this is a cyclical thing. She will grow in confidence only when she sees you taking greater responsibility. If you want a freer hand to do things your way, don't ease off and do less but show her how capable you are of managing.

- Don't forget small children are always difficult to manage. If you're finding it really tough it could be because everybody finds it tough and it's not a reflection of your capabilities.

Can't let go, won't let go

As each partner grows in confidence there is usually a natural sharing of the care of the children. The man begins to adopt some of the responsibility that would have been the woman's in a traditional relationship, and the woman begins to get to grips with some of the responsibilities for financial security that are now hers.

What if that doesn't happen? In other chapters we have discussed the fact that women are conditioned to see their role in their children's lives as a kind of birthright. Some women – perhaps sisters or friends – could be making a life-long career out of the home and family, and sometimes the woman may not want to give any ground at all.

While it is unlikely that a woman would consider role-reversal if she simply could not live with this fact, the territory problem can still surface in many a role-reversed relationship.

While the practicalities of the new situation may be a deciding factor, the realities of the new set-up can feel uncomfortable at first to many women, and they will feel pangs of guilt or resentment. If the woman holds too tightly onto her traditional role and refuses to let her partner take certain responsibilities, the ability to maintain a reversed-role relationship will be limited. So how do you make things work?

There is a whole section on this subject for women in Chapter 3, but if you are a man whose partner is finding it difficult to let go what can you do?

Do's and don'ts for men

- Accept that this issue of territory exists and that it can be difficult to make room for someone else, even if that person is your partner.

- Remember that women are not used to sharing this territory and have few examples around them on which to base their experiences.

- Realize that conditioning is strong and there is an undercurrent around your partner that could be putting pressure on her. Women are often made to feel that they have failed in some way or have rejected their children if they allow their partners to reverse roles with them. This is, of course, without foundation, but still applies pressure.

- Be prepared to discuss what is happening in your relationship.

At the same time:

- Don't try to take too much responsibility too fast.

- Don't allow her to feel left out of the family.

- Don't overrule her at each turn. If you have strong views on how you want to do things, discuss them with her and set out to reach a compromise not get your own way.

- Don't become so wrapped up in your new role that you forget her.

In summary, the role-reversed relationship is unlikely to be more or less difficult to maintain than any other. If there are areas of conflict, they may be different but not necessarily more problematic, so just keep listening, stay flexible and maintain your sense of humour.

CHAPTER 6

What the Experts Say

Ultimately, what anyone else might think about our decision to reverse roles is of little importance. It certainly won't change our minds, but every now and then you will think to yourself, 'Are we doing the right thing? Will it affect the children?'

There was one occasion when my son, who was three at the time, came clopping down the hall in my wife's shoes, with her handbag over his shoulder and said . . . 'I'm off to work now, darling.' My wife and I looked at one another in horror. What had we done?
Paul (47)

To research *Trading Places* we didn't just interview the role-reversed couples themselves. We asked over fifty individuals and leading authorities, including children of reversed-role couples, grans and grandads, health visitors, leading academics, psychologists, sociologists and anyone else we could think of, to give us their views.[1]

We asked them:

- Can fathers look after the home and children as well as mothers can? And do they approach things differently?

- How will it affect the children? Does it give the wrong gender clues?

- Is reversing roles just a fad? Will it die out when the employment situation changes?

WHAT THE EXPERTS SAY

Can fathers look after the children and the house as well as mothers?

Perhaps the best people to ask are the children who have grown-up with Dad in charge.

Dad has been the one at home looking after us for so long that I can't imagine things being any different. Until you mentioned it I hadn't thought it was at all unusual. This idea that men do one thing and women do another is a bit outdated. You should just do what makes you happy? If that's brain-surgery fine, if it's bringing up children, fine.
Siân (17)

I like to have my mum at home but she's not very good at cooking so it's best if Dad cooks. My mum and dad are just the same as they were before dad gave up work. He's still the strict one who tells me off, and Mum helps me with my homework. I think women are probably better at doing the cleaning and things because men are lazier and watch the television all the time.
Naomi (12)

TRADING PLACES

But do men do things differently in the eyes of their offspring?

If mum was there when I got home from school she wouldn't sit and watch the TV like dad does. She would be talking to us more and playing games and things. My mum's job is definitely harder than dad's because she always has marking to do in the evening and doesn't get to sit down until after 9, but Dad can have a break whenever he wants. My dad is really good at organizing things though, like parties or outings and things like that, and my tea's always ready when I get in from school absolutely starving.

Robert (11)

When it comes to grans and grandads, there can sometimes be an element of friction. Many mother-in-laws doubt their son-in-law's ability to cope with a small baby, and some fathers feel disappointed if their sons don't seem to have achieved career success. So what do the parents of couples who reverse roles think about it?

Knowing my daughter it wasn't any surprise to me when they decided my son-in-law would be the one to stay at home with the new baby. She's very ambitious my girl, but she's never wanted to follow in my footsteps when it came to running a home. But she seems to do OK at

WHAT THE EXPERTS SAY

work and my son-in-law manages very well, although I don't always agree with the way he does things, so it seems to work in their case.
Pam (60)

My father has never said so in so many words, but I know he is disappointed that I gave up my career to look after the children. I had a very promising job in R&D, and he finds it very difficult to understand why I was prepared to let that go. I now work with him on a part-time basis and there are no hard feelings.
Mike (34)

For many years, the accepted opinion has been that the mother's relationship with the child has been by far the most important, so how do the people who specialize in this area, see the role of the father?

We are definitely seeing an increasing number of men closely involved in the care of their children, but the situation is by no means clear-cut. In many families, the recession has led to many men working incredibly long hours, giving less support to their wives than, say, ten years ago. While in other families the man may be the primary care-giver. So the way in which the health visitor assists in the early years is changing all the time. One

thing that has been a development in our profession, is the growing number of men entering caring professions, such as nursing, health visiting, etc. This is a positive move, and I see this growing acceptance of a man's value as a care-giver as being important to society as a whole.
Health visitor

It would seem that lecturers in child care are also urging health professionals to account for wider involvement of fathers in their work.

Initially they [child health practitioners] might need to re-examine their attitudes, values and beliefs to explore the changing focus of fathers in today's society. They can enhance the role of fathers by involving them in decisions on care, encouraging them to seek out peers in similar situations and involving them in teaching about child development and child rearing. Increased awareness among practitioners of the importance of the role of fathers can only enhance the opportunity for open debate and strengthen the father's position as joint and equal carer in the family arena.
From 'The Good Father – How is the Role of Fathers in Child Care Changing?'[2]

But although attitudes may be changing, many men, particularly those who are separated from

What the Experts Say

their children because of the breakdown of their relationship, have found that the role of the father is often underestimated. While couples who reverse roles have proved that parents regularly interchange the traditional mother/father roles to suit the best interests of the children, the divorce courts almost always accept the mother's capacity to care for the children as being far superior to the father's.

The best possible arrangement for a child is to live with both parents, but sadly this is not always possible. However, a degree of stereotyping is in operation when judges decide which parent the children should live with after divorce. In 91 per cent of cases the children will live with the mother, with the father being the resident parent on very rare occasions. Much of the incoming legislation affecting the family is gender-neutral, acknowledging that the face of the family has changed entirely in the last 30 to 40 years. Our organization campaigns for a more even balance in the way that the courts consider parenting roles and urges those involved in the divorce process to look beyond the obvious stereotype before arriving at a decision affecting families.

Ian Mackay, Families Need Fathers

And is there any psychological reason fathers shouldn't be the 'primary care-giver', as the term goes?

For a long time it was believed that babies formed just one 'primary attachment' (usually with their mothers) on which their emotional health depended . . . However we now know that tiny infants develop simultaneous attachments with anyone in regular cooing distance. A father doesn't interrupt a more significant attachment between mother and child, and his function in infant development is not secondary to hers unless circumstance (or his own desire) makes it so.
Adrienne Burgess, Research Fellow at the Institute for Public Research Policy[3]

Men may approach parenthood in a different way from women, but difference doesn't equal deficit. Issues of masculinity and femininity are increasingly clouded and within this men are re-evaluating their roles in the lives of their children. Perhaps the best way to answer the question is to define why the percentage of highly involved fathers is not higher.

I see three problems which prevent men from developing closer relationships with their children, and these issues may have been considered by men who are primary care-givers. First, fathers who get directly

What the Experts Say

involved with children in a way that resembles mothers (if not exactly identical to it) are often worried about being thought effeminate, something they have learned to associate with being gay. Second, fear of femininity itself, of losing the privileges of masculinity and being swallowed up in an abject maternal swamp. Third, many men have told me of what amounts to fear of death stemming from the need to stay still, being rather than doing, that is a part of relating to and looking after children. Male identity depends so much on movement 'out there' that the home comes to feel like a tomb.

Andrew Samuels, Professor of Analytical Psychology at the University of Essex and a psychotherapist with extensive experience of working with men

How will it affect the children?

Will there be any lasting effects on your children if they are brought up mainly by dad while mum is at work?

Your mum and dad are exactly the same people, whatever they do during the day, so it sort of doesn't make any difference who does the washing and the cooking, and who earns the money. For example, when I was little I

preferred my mum to be around if I was ill, and I know that she's the strictest one while Dad's more laid-back. That wouldn't have been any different if Dad was away at work all day, because their personalities would still be the same.
Alex (13)

In fact, there is an increasingly convincing body of evidence to suggest that children brought up mainly by their fathers progress even more successfully, as they receive a kind of 'double investment'. Typically, working mothers devote more 'quality time' to their children when they get in from work than a working man and spend a smaller percentage of their free time on hobbies that take them away from the home and family. Add this to the attention of a full-time dad, and you can see that the children of role-reversed couples appear to get a 'double dose' of attention during their most important school years.[4]

Should we be concerned that children are picking up the wrong clues about gender? Will they be confused in later life about what it is like to be male and how you should act if you're female?

What the Experts Say

Sex role conditioning floods in from everywhere as a child develops. The sense of sexual identity is not solely based on the relationship of the child's parents. In fact, if the parents have reversed roles and seem to contravene the norm, the child is likely to develop a broader understanding of the possibilities open to both sexes. Pre-school children, particularly, play at being both male and female – in fact they spend a fair bit of time pretending to be cats or dogs with equal enthusiasm, so parents could be worrying unnecessarily if their little boy wants to wear make-up like mummy. There are types of parental behaviour which can impact on the child's sexual identity, but simply reversing roles is not a significant factor in this process.[5]

Is reversing roles just a fad?

Is the current employment situation driving couples to reverse roles or are we all searching for the best way to keep the family happy without going bankrupt? Are role-reversed partners dual-earner families who couldn't take the pace or are they pioneers of a completely new way of life? We asked a leading expert in family policy studies to interpret how work and family go together.

The factors influencing the employment and domestic roles adopted by parental couples are complex: some are located in the private sphere of personal behaviour, expectations and values, others in the economic and social context of family life. In our recent study of 6000 mothers and fathers aged 33, there is little evidence to suggest that full-time employment of both parents is linked to an erosion of family life. It is long hours (particularly when fathers work more than 50 hours per week) rather than the fact of employment itself which have a detrimental effect.

Dr Elsa Ferri, Senior Research Fellow and lecturer at City University

Perhaps for many of us, the recognition that no employer will ever put our family life first, has driven us to take that responsibility out of their hands. It may be not so much *whether* you work but for *how long*. No matter how plentiful the jobs may become, if the employer expects you to chase around the country for over 50 hours a week, the pay will never be enough to make up for the damage it would do to family life.

It looks as if, for many couples, there will always be the conflicting interests of career and family life, with many children losing out to the demands of an employer and the need for

What the Experts Say

financial security. There will always be a huge number of families who follow a traditional pattern, but that will not suit us all.

Reversing roles may not be driven by changes in society and the employment situation as might first appear. Many couples have assessed their priorities and decided that enough is enough and that only so many sacrifices can be made. Whether the aim is greater freedom from a 9-to-5 job, more involvement in your family life or simply an arrangement that allows the best use of the individual personalities of those involved, this is an alternative lifestyle that is chosen by an increasing number of couples.

Having stumbled, almost by chance on reversing roles, we may have actually found a solution to the age-old conflict between career and family. Research indicates that, in limiting the impact of long working hours on the family, we may be providing a better environment than the dual-earner format, which would have been the next best alternative.

CHAPTER 7

Protecting Your Rights

Reversing roles may be the best option for the children, but it is not likely to fill your bank manager with delight. Unless you have a very high income or significant savings, finances are likely to be a struggle at times. It is more important than ever that you protect your interests. Obviously, you have to get the maximum cash flow on a monthly basis, but what many couples overlook is their long-term financial security.

So where can you save money and which areas should you look at carefully when you reverse roles?

PROTECTING YOUR RIGHTS

- Taxation – the Married Couples' Allowance can be transferred to the wife's salary or shared across both to ensure you receive all tax relief to which you are entitled.

- National Insurance Contributions – arrangements can be made to prevent a man from missing out on National Insurance Contributions if he is caring for the children, but this will not happen automatically.

- Pension rights – moving out of full-time employment can affect your pension rights, and although you may want to continue your contributions to the fund there may be restrictions on you doing so.

- Life assurance – should you review your cover if your work arrangements change?

- Bank charges and overdraft facilities – how do you get the best from your bank?

- Debts – Are you stuck with your debts or would you benefit from shopping around?

- Savings – will reversing roles be the end of saving or can you benefit as a non tax-payer?

Taxation

If you are reducing your family income to one income, it makes sense to check that you are receiving any tax relief to which you may be entitled. This is particularly true of the Married Couple's Allowance, which is transferable between husband and wife.

Married couples

Since 6 April 1993 it has been possible for the allowance to be given to the wife or split between both partners. You can do this whatever the level of your income.

Ask your Tax Office for a Form 18 to complete and return. It will need to be told what you want to happen before the start of the new tax year on 6 April. The figure will be shown, not as an amount of income you can receive without paying tax, but as a lump sum reduction from the wife's total tax figure.

Once you have done this, the change will apply until you decide to alter it. You do not need to complete a new form every year. If you do want to alter it, the new arrangement will take effect at the start of the tax year after you have told the Tax Office about the change.

Unmarried couples

The man's Personal Allowance cannot be transferred, but a woman who has a child of up to 16 (or 21 in full-time education) living with her, and is unmarried, legally separated or divorced, can claim a dependants allowance. This is the same amount as the Married Person's Allowance.

National Insurance Contributions

To get the full rate of basic retirement pension, you normally need to have enough contributions in about $9/10$ths of your working life. The Department of Social Security takes a person's working life as 49 years (age 16 to 65) for a woman and 49 years (age 16 to 65) for a man.

If you spend a significant amount of time looking after the children you will lose the 'stamp', which would normally be provided to you free of charge when claiming Unemployment Benefit/ Job Seeker's Allowance. There is, therefore, a danger that you will, over time, fall behind the level of NI contributions that should have been paid.

The Department of Social Security has a scheme called Home Responsibilities Protection (HRP), by which a man can be credited with NI contributions. You will not necessarily be advised of this and you will not automatically receive these credits, so you should look into this scheme and claim anything to which you are entitled.

You can get HRP for any complete tax year, after April 1978, if you were the main payee getting Child Benefit for a child under 16. HRP is automatically credited to a woman if she has been getting Child Benefit for a child under 16 during a year in which she has not paid sufficient NI contributions but as, in most cases, the Child Benefit is in the woman's name, men can lose out.

A man, whether married or single, can get Child Benefit only if he produces a signed statement from his partner that says that she does not wish to claim that benefit. This may seem rather extraordinary, but it is probably a safeguard for women who could otherwise find their Child Benefit riding on the favourite in the 2.15 at Newmarket.

The conditions, particularly if you work part time or have self-employed earnings, are relatively complex, but this is definitely something you need to look into.

The guidance leaflet you need is Leaflet NP 27, which is entitled 'Looking after someone at home? How to protect your pension'. The scheme to refer to is Home Responsibilities Protection (HRP).

Your local Benefits Agency office should be able to provide the leaflet and advice, but you will probably find that you will have to liaise with the Child Benefit Centre in Newcastle upon Tyne to make final arrangements.

Pension rights

Home Responsibilities Protection can prevent a man from missing out on his state pension, but if you were part of an employer's pension scheme or have a Personal Pension Plan, then everything will change when you give up work. You can continue to pay into pension schemes of this type only if you have a source of earned income. If you work part time there is no problem, because you can have a Personal Pension Plan, but if you have no paid employment, contributions to the pension fund will have to stop until you resume employment.

You will not, of course, lose out on what you have already paid in to the scheme. In most cases this will be held by the pension company and 'deferred' until you reach normal retirement age. What you have to consider carefully is how you will make sure that your long-term financial needs can be catered for in the absence of a fully paid-up pension.

A good starting point is to seek independent financial advice to assess how things stand at the moment. Most schemes holding deferred pension benefit will probably increase in value (without further contributions) at a rate of up to 5 per cent per annum. This is a positive move in the right direction, but a few years of high inflation will see any increase in that value wiped out in real terms. Exceptions, of course, are many public sector pension schemes, which are index-linked. The financial adviser should be able to help you understand your current situation and explain the options that are open to you.

How can you fill the pensions gap?

Married couples

If you are married and your wife belongs to an employer's scheme, she could opt to make Additional Voluntary Contributions (AVCs) into her pension fund to provide a greater degree of financial security later on. There are in-house AVCs and free-standing AVCs, which can replace the shortfall left by the husband's pension. The same applies if the wife has a Personal Pension Plan as she can ask advice and increase the amount paid in to the fund to make up the difference.

You may feel that there are disadvantages here, though. This arrangement could prove to be less than ideal in the event of a divorce. With the pension paying-out in the wife's name, the husband is left with little claim on the funds should you decide to part company. A man would have to debate his rights to the funds in court.

An alternative route would be for the man to build up a fund in his own name by a different form of savings plan. Obviously, the pension scheme has a higher potential pay-back than many other options, as it works with pre-tax income, but in the absence of this, schemes such as

Personal Equity Plans, TESSAs (or their replacements) or Unit Trusts could fill the gap. In addition they may give the kind of flexibility that many couples now require. As many people retire early, before the due date for their pension, these more flexible options could provide a welcome addition to a traditional pension scheme.

Unmarried couples

If you are living together, the cohabitee can be named as beneficiary of any death benefits within a personal pension. If you belong to an employer's scheme, however, you need to make contact with the trustees of the scheme to check that the rules permit this.

If you are unmarried of course, there is no guarantee under current law that the man will benefit from the woman's pension at all in the event of the relationship breaking down in later life. If the man has little or no pension to pay out in the future, life could be extremely hard. Men can be faced with some of the financial problems which have traditionally concerned women. Once again, a different form of stand-alone savings plan in the man's could be considered.

Life assurance

An area that is easy to overlook when you reverse roles is the life assurance protection your family might need.

If one of you leaves employment the family can stand to lose out in a number of different ways. You would no longer be covered by the statutory life assurance provided by your employer. On leaving the employer's pension scheme, you also lose certain life assurance benefits. For example, a pension scheme could pay up to four times the salary in the event of the holder dying before the full term of the pension. It is likely that a widow's pension of up to two-thirds of salary would also be paid, and some schemes include a pension for dependants, so you are losing a number of contingency benefits at once. Many employers also offer private medical insurance or other health-related benefits as part of the package, which you may wish to replace from your own money.

When you reverse roles it would probably be worth seeking independent financial advice to make sure that you are adequately covered for life assurance and other 'worst scenario' protection, such as financial help in the event of critical illness or mortgage protection if the main earner should lose her job.

Before we move on to less depressing subjects, it is probably best to mention that it is advisable to have an up-to-date will, particularly if you are unmarried, as some areas such as transfer of property are not as straightforward as you might think.

Banks

One experience of men who have reversed roles is that a bank that has previously treated them as valued customers suddenly turns rather unfriendly. Most branches are used to dealing with men who regularly deposit funds. When the salary cheques no longer arrive, your credit-rating can plummet, and the bank's approach may be rather more cool and distant than you would like.

Much of this springs from the fact that banks have to make basic assumptions to decide how to manage lending, and in the eyes of a bank manager, the long-term unemployed and the growing band of house-husbands are pretty much the same thing. While the rest of society may be waking up to the idea of reversing roles, the norm in banking circles is for men to earn. A number of men have experienced sudden withdrawal of overdraft facilities, unpleasant letters and arm's length treatment from previously helpful and courteous bank personnel.

It appears there is a simple solution. Take the time to visit your branch to explain your new circumstances. Make clear how you intend to manage your finances in the future and give your bank the chance to see that this is a considered and responsible decision rather than an unpleasant downturn in your monetary affairs. If you and your partner have separate accounts, they may not necessarily be seeing your accounts together, and this will give them a chance to build a full picture.

This should put an end to any nervousness on the bank's part, although house-husbands shouldn't hold out too much hope on the large overdraft front. Most importantly though, the person you speak to will be able to advise you on the most appropriate of their services to keep your bank charges to a minimum, and they will be able to organize any movement of direct debits, standing orders and so on that need to be realigned for a single income.

In time, the banking profession, along with many other areas of our daily life, will, we hope, get more used to full-time dads.

Debts

Debts such as mortgages, credit cards and personal loans are often unavoidable, but you should shop around to see if you are getting the best possible deal.

A useful exercise is to check the annual percentage rate (APR) of a range of credit cards and consider moving to one that helps you to pay back your debt more quickly with less accumulated interest. Some companies even offer incentives for giving them your credit card debts. It's a crazy world, but if you shop around you could make real reductions in your monthly outgoings.

The same goes for mortgages, where it is sometimes possible to move to a more advantageous package, perhaps with lower interest rates and/or cash-back arrangements. Be careful to look at the penalties your existing company will impose, and do your calculations based on the full picture. Many mortgages will impose a charge for giving up the mortgage before the end of the 25-year period. Don't forget to inspect all the small print to check that what seems to be a bargain is genuine and that you won't end up paying over the odds in the future. Once again, an independent financial adviser should be able to help you.

Savings

One area where you may actually benefit from having no income is when it comes to savings. If you are a non-tax-payer you do not have to pay tax on interest from savings in deposit and building society accounts. Fill in an Inland Revenue R85 form if you would like to receive gross payment of interest or open an account that pays gross interest automatically. Don't forget that the account cannot be held in joint names if one of you is employed.

Your personal allowance is taken into consideration when you receive interest, so you will be able to receive up to this amount in interest before you become liable. This does not affect Married Couple's Allowance.

There are also benefits if you own shares. Companies pay tax on dividends before forwarding this sum to you, so non-tax-payers can reclaim the tax deducted (which at the time of writing was 20 per cent).

Both partners will have their own capital gains tax allowances, so this is unaffected if you do not pay income tax.

Financial issues are constantly changing, with each budget affecting your circumstances to a greater or lesser degree. Keep in touch with changes and make sure that you benefit from the insight of an independent financial adviser at regular intervals. And, although this may not be the most prosperous time of your life, you can make sure that you are not making things difficult for yourselves in the future.

Information compiled with the assistance of John Gaskell BA (Econ) FIFP CFP

CHAPTER 8

Role Reversal and Early Retirement

Much of this book has looked at couples with young children, but this is just one part of the picture. The recent trends for younger and younger people to retire, and for redundancies to be sought among senior members of staff have led to a very high number of couples renegotiating their breadwinner/housework contract in middle age, often after many years of marriage.

Testing times

Many couples now in their fifties probably did not consider the possibility of reversing roles in the early stages of the relationship. The trend towards early retirement is a relatively recent one, and culturally, there were few full-time fathers to act as role models when we were growing up.

Couples in a partnership of such long standing may have operated for many years with a set of understandings that have now been completely replaced. These changes, often enforced by employers, may not be altogether welcome, and it can, for many reasons, be more difficult to reverse roles at this stage in the relationship than, for example, for a couple in their late twenties. There are several factors at work.

- When you first get together, the relationship goes through many changes as you get used to one another or when the children are born. Reversing roles at this time becomes part of an ongoing process. After many years together, patterns are clearly set and things may have continued for some time without significant alteration. Reversing roles can therefore be a tremendous upheaval.

Role Reversal and Early Retirement

- Conditioning in terms of what men and women should do can be even more difficult to abandon. Many women will have grown up thinking that women shouldn't work but will have found that they can and do have careers after marriage and now find themselves as sole bread-winner. An enormous amount of flexibility is needed to make this transition. Men in this age group may have been encouraged to see their success as inextricably linked to their earning capacity, and being without a pay packet can come hard.

- Many couples have a way of working out their relationship that has proved to be successful. They may have seen other relationships fail around them, while their own has remained stable. There can be a fear of the unknown involved in reversing roles, and many couples may not want to risk a winning formula for an untested arrangement.

- Men are often left with a feeling of 'unfinished business'. They may find it difficult to come to terms with the new situation, and although they are actually retired the reality of not returning to full-time work can be difficult to absorb.

- Women who have carried out household tasks day in, day out for year after year can find it difficult to adapt to a different way of doing things. It can seem like a personal slight if the husband decides to do things in his own way, and feelings can be hurt.

- Financial arrangements may have been made with retirement at 65 as the goal. Many couples find themselves faced with a gaping hole between early retirement and the pension being paid. This may mean that the woman works full time when previously she worked part time or that she is unable to retire early. These financial pressures can put an enormous strain on the relationship.

Nevertheless, couples who reverse roles because of early retirement can be in a stronger position to renegotiate their roles than a younger couple for several reasons.

- Over time you develop ways of sorting out your differences of opinion, and this ability to resolve conflict is extremely important when you reverse roles.

- When you are in your twenties career ambitions and family responsibilities can be in continual conflict. Many couples facing early retirement will have achieved much of what they set out to achieve in their careers and may have a certain independence from their children who are older, so a major source of conflict is out of the way.

- The relationship has already experienced adapting to meet new environments. It may have successfully weathered various storms, and that is an indication that it can take another life change in its stride.

- The ability to adapt to new circumstances has nothing to do with age. It depends on your attitude. A 25-year-old may find it more difficult to be flexible than a 55-year-old because of their approach or personality. You are not at a disadvantage when it comes to reversing roles just because of your age.

Many thousands of couples can and do renegotiate their roles because of early retirement and in doing so discover a new energy to regard it not as the beginning of the end for their personal aspirations but as the end of the beginning, with a new and exciting phase to come.

At first we were all doom and gloom, but then, when we started to change things, we discovered that it was just

TRADING PLACES

what our relationship needed. We had fallen into a bit of a rut and now we're viewing our future with much more enthusiasm.

Daphne (54), school nurse

The period leading up to my redundancy was extremely stressful. To be really honest I was devastated by it. I had always been a company man. If there was a sacrifice to be made in my family life then I would make it. When I saw that the company had every intention of throwing me on the scrap-heap . . . well, I was disgusted. At first I took it personally and felt really let down, but then I started to get angry, and eventually I sat down and completely re-evaluated what I wanted out of life. Suddenly all the sacrifices I had made didn't need to be made any more, and I could put myself and Barbara first for once. At the time I thought it was a tragedy, but now I'm pleased that it happened. Our lives are much happier.

Peter (58), ex-sales manager

But not everyone feels so comfortable with the situation.

I'm just glad my father's not alive. I struggle with the idea of pushing a vacuum cleaner round while my wife's at work, but he would turn in his grave!

George (58), ex-printer

Role Reversal and Early Retirement

How can you make things go more smoothly?

- Treat it as the beginning of a new phase and approach it with optimism and enthusiasm. If you greet the changes positively, with an open mind, it will be easier to feel at home in your new lifestyle.

- Keep talking. When you've lived with someone for most of your adult life it's easy to assume that they know what you're thinking. Nobody's that psychic. Keep the lines of communication open.

- Try to see your circumstances as permanent for the foreseeable future. Things won't change overnight, but they will have to change. Accept that the process of change has begun and try to look further forwards into your long-term future. It's all too easy to feel, subconsciously, that you have unfinished business to attend to. As soon as you sever these lingering feelings of responsibility as an employee the sooner you will be able to shape your new life.

- Be kind to yourself. There's no point wishing that things were different, and it is easy to blame yourself. Make up your mind to change things or resolve to get used to them, but don't hanker after what might have been.

- Consider seeking expert advice if your finances are worrying you or you have a gap before your pension is paid. An independent financial adviser will help you to decide among a number of options. This is also important if you want a redundancy payment to go as far as possible.

- Look at how you will reschedule your lives. When one of you retires early you may find yourselves changing old habits to fit in with your new lifestyle.

And now for some don'ts:

- Don't forget that society is changing. Increasing numbers of early retirers with more time on their hands has changed the way we look at our middle years. There are more opportunities for early retirers than our parents would have thought possible. Don't feel self-conscious about grabbing these new experiences with both hands.

- Don't panic if your partner starts to change the habits of a lifetime. If your husband buys a wok and starts cooking bean-shoots, let him. If your wife signs up for an evening class in advanced mathematics, then don't pour cold water on it. Give each other room to experiment with new interests and activities, which may or may not become part of your new life. Later, it may be out with the mathematics and in with nineteenth-century philosophy, but give each other space to try new things.

- Don't cling too tightly to things that you have outgrown. If a pattern no longer seems to fit in, don't worry too much about replacing it with something else.

- Don't assume that your own retirement will be a carbon copy of your father's or your mother's. Things are very different now. It is not so much that retirement has been brought forward. Instead an additional phase needs to be fitted in, and you are free to decide how to develop your life.

CHAPTER 9

Where to from Here?

We have looked at what reversing roles can be like for each of the partners, taken some time to understand what happens within the relationship, dealt with some potential problems, given our finances a work-out and asked the experts what they had to say. All that remains now is to give you some final information that may be useful.

If you decide you want to make contact with other dads and form your own network, here are some general pointers on getting something like this off the ground. Lastly, the names and addresses of a few organizations that can help are listed on page 185.

Where to from Here?

Forming a local network

Some men are quite happy with their own company and can't imagine anything worse than meeting up with other full-time dads. If you would rather have some adult company now and again, however, away from the mothers and toddlers scene, the chances are that you may have to take the initiative.

The figures indicate that 17 men in every 1000 are full-time fathers,[1] so they are out there somewhere, although tracking them down may be difficult. There are several ways you might be able to find out who else is pacing the streets with a buggy for want of something more interesting to do. You could try one of the following:

- Display a small poster at the clinic, doctor's surgery, local school, sports centre, village hall notice board, library, post office and so on inviting other full-time dads to get in touch.

- Rely on word of mouth. Mention that you're interested in getting together with other house-husbands to friends, neighbours, health visitors and so forth. You'll be surprised at how effective this can be. (Many of the interviewees for this book were tracked down this way.)

- Make sure the mothers' networks know what you are trying to do. Local branches of the National Childbirth Trust (NCT) or Meet-A-Mum Association might be able to pass on information to a wider group of parents with young children. The NCT occasionally organizes ante-natal classes and groups for dads, so this is another possibility.

- Use the local media. Our experience is that local newspapers and radio can be supportive of people trying to launch new local community initiatives. They might provide you with much-needed free publicity if approached correctly, and the wide readership/listenership will help you to reach a wider audience very quickly. Be prepared for them to be interested in your personal circumstances if the subject really captures their imagination. There is still a novelty value attached to full-time dads, and profiles of house-husbands are popular features in local newspapers. You could be asked to speak on local radio or be photographed washing-up! Make sure you do only as much as you feel comfortable with to promote the cause.

Where to from Here?

- Take the initiative and try to arrange an activity to which other full-time dads can be invited. Would a local sports centre or gym be interested in putting an hour aside in their schedule for men with children? Would a local country house hotel or child-friendly restaurant like to play host during an otherwise quiet time of the week? You will never know unless you ask. If you work closely with your local media to tell them what is happening you may even be able to arrange a free listing in the 'What's On' section.

If you decide to reverse roles, congratulations on your decision and best wishes for the future. And if you're already a seasoned campaigner with a good few years of reversing roles under your belt, we hope that the thoughts and reminiscences of everyone who contributed to this book will have struck a chord with your own experiences of 'Trading Places'.

References

Chapter 1

1 The Barrass Company, *Genderquake, Programme 3*, Channel 4, 1996

2 Sly, F., 'Mothers in the Labour Market', *Employment Gazette*, London, November 1994

3 Laurence, C., 'Honey I'll Look After the Kids', *Daily Telegraph*, London, 22 January 1997

4 Ferri, E., *Britain's 33-Year-Olds – The Fifth Follow-up to the National Child Development Study*, Economic & Social Research Council/ National Children's Bureau, London, 1993

5 The Barrass Company, *Genderquake*, Channel 4, 1996

6 The 'Trading Places' opinion survey was conducted with 76 adults (38 couples) in which the man had primary responsibility for

the children and the home, either at present or in the past. A total of 58 questionnaires were completed during in-depth interviews, with the remaining eighteen supplied and returned by post. Of this sample, 34 couples were married and four were cohabiting. All the couples had children.

The age range for women was as follows:

20–29 years:	10.5 per cent
30–39 years:	47.5 per cent
40–49 years:	37 per cent
50–59 years:	5 per cent

The age range for men was as follows:

20–29 years:	0 per cent
30–39 years:	58 per cent
40–49 years:	31.5 per cent
50–59 years:	10.5 per cent

The longest amount of time spent as primary care giver was 17 years, and the shortest time was one year. The highest percentage of those interviewed had spent more than five years as primary care giver. The classification of primary care giver was based on where responsibility lay and did not eliminate those men involved in home-based self-employment, part-time work or full-time study, when their partners were full-time workers.

Children of the couples interviewed ranged in age from newborn to 22 years. Of these children, 60 per cent were boys and 40 per cent girls.

In terms of employment, of those men interviewed, 14 were full-time house-husbands, two were mature students, ten were self-employed, ten were working in part-time jobs and two were in early retirement.

Those who completed questionnaires were from London, Oxfordshire, Cambridgeshire, Devon, Norfolk and Greater Manchester.

The sample, while fitting designated classification criteria, should not be seen as representative of all reversed-role couples throughout the UK. More data on age, geographical spread, family size and employment status of this sector of society would be necessary before a fully representative survey could be held.

REFERENCES

Chapter 6

1   Some of those approached for statistics and opinions on role-reversal were:

Adrienne Burgess – Research Fellow and author of *Fatherhood Reclaimed*

At Home Dads – US-based support group

City College, Health & Social Studies Department

City University – Dr Elsa Ferri

Central Statistical Office

Centre for Policy Studies

Demos

Economic & Social Research Council

ECN Pensioners Association

Families Need Fathers

Family Policies Studies Centre

MCPHVA – Mary Daley

Institute for Employment Studies, University of Sussex

Institute for Public Policy Research – Jane Franklin

National Childbirth Trust – Clodagh Corcoran

Norwich Young Fathers Group – Justin Wolf

Parentline

Relate – Julia Cole

University of East Anglia – Professor John Gubbay, Lecturer in gender, class and race in the School of Social Studies

University of Essex – Andrew Samuels, Professor of Analytical Psychology

2. 'The Good Father – How is the Role of Fathers in Child Care Changing?' published in *Child Health* magazine June/July 1994. Authors: Sarah Baker BEd, RGN, RSCN, RHV, DipHS (Childcare Lecturer, Kingston and St George's NHS College of Health Studies) and Margaret Lane MSc, RSCN, RCNT, DipNEd (Senior Lecturer in Childcare, St Bartholomew's and Princess Alexandra and Newham College of Nursing and Midwifery).

REFERENCES

3   Burgess, Adrienne (Research Fellow at the Institute for Public Research Policy), *Fatherhood Reclaimed*, Vermilion, London, 1997

4   Burgess, A., op. cit.

5   Burgess, A., op. cit.

Chapter 9

1   Sly, F., op. cit.

Useful addresses

An American group, At Home Dads, has set up a web-site and quarterly newsletter, which you might like to investigate. The Internet address is:

http://www.familyinternet.com/dad/dad.htm

If you don't have access to the Internet but want to find out more about the newsletter you can contact:

At Home Dads
61 Drightwood Avenue
North Andover
Massachusetts 01845
USA

USEFUL ADDRESSES

Closer to home a new organization is hoping to set up a national information centre for full-time dads. You can contact it on:

H^2 (pronounced H-squared)
Georgian House
North Walsham Road
Happisburgh
Norfolk
NR12 0QS

Tel: 01692 651522

A couple of organizations that organize workshops and groups for fathers on an ad hoc basis are:

National Childbirth Trust
Alexandra House
Oldham Terrace
London
W3 6NH

Tel: 0181 992 8637

The NCT has over 400 branches nationwide, and in some areas there are also fathers' groups.

Parent Network
44 Caversham Road
London
NW5 2DS

Tel: 0171 485 8535

The Network provides support for parents and training workshops on parenting skills. A number of local groups is in operation, run specifically by fathers, for fathers.

Several other organizations exist to provide support in difficult circumstances:

Families Need Fathers
National Office
134 Curtain Road
London
EC2A 3AR

Information: 0181 886 0970
Helpline: 0891 448690 (unmarried)
Helpline: 0891 448696 (married)

This is a self-help organization and registered charity whose primary concern is to maintain a child's relationship with both parents during and following divorce or separation.

USEFUL ADDRESSES

Relate Marriage Guidance
National Headquarters
Herbert Gray College
Little Church Street
Rugby CV21 3AP

Tel: 01788 573241

Relate offers counselling for couples. There are 130 centres in England, Wales and Northern Ireland; see the telephone directory for your local centre.

Parentline
Endway House
The Endway
Hadleigh
Essex SS7 2AN

Tel: 01702 559900

This is a 24-hour helpline for distressed parents; see the telephone directory for your local group.

Also available in Vista paperback

All by Myself
SAMANTHA LEE

When your man walks out it may be cold comfort to realize that you are not alone. There is an ever-growing army of abandoned women out there. Women trying to cope not only with rejection, but also with the vagaries of a frequently unworkable and notoriously unsupportive social security system – while their other halves go on their merry ways rejoicing. Women like Samantha Lee, whose partner of twenty-five years suddenly left her for another woman. Through this initially devastating experience she managed to overcome the bad times and to see them as an opportunity to build an even better life for herself.

At whatever stage your relationship fell apart, her uplifting and essentially down-to-earth advice will show you how to readjust emotionally, practically and triumphantly to single life.

She survived, and so will you. All by yourself.

ISBN 0 575 60083 7

Solved by Sunset
How to solve a problem in 24 hours or less

CAROL ORSBORN

Are you frustrated with a problem that you just can't seem to resolve? Sometimes trying to master an issue logically simply makes things worse. So why not stop trying to make things happen and find room for creativity and inspiration?

Solved by Sunset will teach you how to create a turning point in any long-term difficulty by balancing the rational qualities of your left-brain thinking with the intuition and imagination of your right.

All you need is paper, pen and a dilemma. Then set aside just one day from your busy schedule and, by following the steps oulined, you will learn how to put things in perspective, re-evaluate your goals – and look forward to a trouble-free sunrise!

ISBN 0 575 60165 5

VISTA

Feng Shui for Lovers
SARAH BARTLETT

Feng Shui is the ancient Oriental art of arranging objects in order to maximize the energy (*ch'i*) and harmony inherent in the environment.

Practical and fun, by using such energizers as lights, plants and mirrors, Feng Shui can enrich your relationships and create enjoyment in all aspects of your personal world.

Whether your aim is to attract a new love, hang on to the old one or reboost your sex life; or whether you live in a mansion, a flat, or just a room to yourself, by applying the basic principles of Feng Shui you can simply, cheaply and quickly bring magic back into your home – and your relationships – for ever.

ISBN 0 575 60137 X

VISTA